Shattered Shackles
200 True Stories of Individuals Receiving Freedom Through Jesus Christ

Robert J. Hammond & Karen E. Hammond

2023

All rights reserved. No part of this publication may be produced or transmitted in any form or by any means, electronic or mechanical, including photocopying, recording, or otherwise, without permission in writing from this publisher.

ISBN   979-8-218-14839-3

Front cover illustration design by Jessica Davis

These authors may be contacted to order more books, to minister deliverance, or to schedule speaking engagements and conferences at: shatteredshacklesministry@gmail.com or call 270-392-4976 or 270-392-8499.

Website: www.shatteredshackles.com

@2023 This Moment Publishers

Table of Contents

Acknowledgements 4

Introduction 5

Chapter 1 – Demons Speaking Through People 11

Chapter 2 – Sex Spirits 32

Chapter 3 – Suicide Spirits 50

Chapter 4 – False Gods 60

Chapter 5 – Rejection Spirits 69

Chapter 6 – Witchcraft and the Occult 83

Chapter 7 – Generational Iniquity 101

Chapter 8 – Spirits of Infirmity 112

Chapter 9 – Casting Out By the Spoken Word 127

Chapter 10 – Casting Demons Off Of People 136

Chapter 11 – Individuals Under 20 Years Old 144

Chapter 12 – Haunted Homes 156

Chapter 13 – Anger Spirits 164

Chapter 14 – Miscellaneous 177

Chapter 15 – Minimal Results 192

Chapter 16 – Conclusion: Now What? 199

About the Authors 203

Bibliography 204

Acknowledgements

All praise and glory to Jesus Christ who has made it possible for all of us to come into relationship with Him through His blood which was shed on the cross for us. Additionally, we thank and praise the Holy Spirit for leading us into the understanding of the power we as followers of Jesus have and can exercise in our daily walk as Christians. Thank you, Jesus, for giving us the authority to trample on all the powers of the enemy, thereby being able to provide freedom to those who are oppressed of the devil.

Thank you to the many individuals who have shared their stories of deliverance and freedom which they have received through Christ. This book would not have happened without your willingness and openness to contribute to this manuscript.

Thank you to Mom and Dad Wassom for praying for us, supporting us and encouraging us to continue to move forward as God leads us in ministry. Particularly to Dad for telling us it was time to share this information that others may receive freedom through Christ. We absolutely knew it was God's timing.

Thank you for the many individuals who have been and are a part of *Shattered Shackles Ministry* and are committed to helping others receive the freedom in Christ which they have experienced.

Introduction

I (Bob) had only intended to publish one book, and that took some urging. Some have suggested I write a book on the purpose of the four Gospels (Matthew-King, Mark-Servant, Luke-Son of Man, John-Son of God) while others thought I should do one on my STUDY project from the gospels, "What Would Jesus Do?" But I never felt led by the Spirit to do these.

Recently, I thought about compiling testimonies of deliverance from evil spirits. I chewed on it and asked the Lord if I should and waited for an answer. I casually mentioned it to my father-in-law. His response was unlike anything he has ever said to me. "Bob!" He waited until I looked at him before he continued, "You need to do this book!" It didn't feel like Dad Wassom was speaking to me! It was more like First Lieutenant Earl E. Wassom ordering a crew member of his B-24 bomber in World War II! I don't remember what I said, but I wanted to salute with, "Yes sir!" That is the moment I decided to do this project.

I have found that people are very interested in true stories of demons and deliverance and when they hear or read them, they become interested in receiving the same or speaking to someone they know who needs it. The purpose of sharing these is that people will have a better understanding of deliverance and will receive the same freedom these individuals have experienced as a result of going through the ministry of deliverance. Who knows how many will be touched by these stories and how many of them Jesus will eventually set free!

This book gives specific accounts of individuals being set free from personal torments such as anxiety, suicide, sex addictions, anger, PTSD, depression, fear, rejection and other life limiting problems. Jesus has come to set the captives free (Luke 4:18).

Over the years, we've done deliverance with people who are rich, poor, famous, mega-church pastors, highly educated, uneducated, lead singers on national Christian TV broadcasts, have been on "paranormal" TV shows and from numerous countries on five continents. There is a common thread: God is not a respecter of person and loves all His people equally!

Clarifications

For confidentiality reasons, some names, locations and other identifiable characteristics have been changed at the request of the individuals to maintain their anonymity. No details involving the deliverances have been changed in any way, so that you are reading true, factual accounts. However, if a story starts with, "My name is Bubba Smith," then you know that Bubba Smith is the person's real name. Some of these accounts have been written by individuals overseas and you may see some incorrect English, which have been left in for authenticity.

About 90% of the stories I (Bob) was personally involved with. The other 10% are from people I know well and am certain that the stories they wrote are true and accurate.

Many times the authors are anonymous (including me). This is intentional because we want God to get the glory and not the people writing, unless they are telling their own story and are willing to put their heart out there and be publicly honest about their mistakes in life.

In some stories, you will read terms like Transformation Seminar, Inner Healing and Deliverance Seminar, Deliverance Weekend or Freedom Weekend. When Transformation seminar or Inner Healing is read, they refer to the two-week classes we did in India and the stories are written by Indians. Transformation Weekend or Freedom Weekend refers to the three-day deliverances we do here in the United States for both small and large groups.

At times, in testimonies, you will see that the individuals state that they stopped all their medication and are healed. We at NO time encourage individuals to stop any prescription medication; we actually tell them to speak with their physicians to determine if they should or not.

If, as a follower of Christ, you are under bondage to secret sin, and if you are not living in His freedom, you will see from these true accounts that you can live the free and abundant life Jesus promises the believer. This book will open your eyes to the power of Jesus' name.

Story #1 is the first of 200 because it is well written and gives a good recap to the reader about how a Freedom Weekend flows.

Ministry History

It all started in the fall of 1979 (story #2). With that experience, I (Bob) was determined to find out about evil spirits (demons) and how to get them out of people. The journey was long and arduous as I studied every Scripture in the Bible about demons/evil spirits/the devil. It was interesting, educational and even shocking as I discovered a voluminous amount of helpful information that I had no idea was there! Furthermore, Jesus, the Head of the Body, put situations in my path to help me learn. When the opportunity came, I always knew just enough to help someone get free until I eventually had my first experience of actually casting a demon out of someone (story #111). I could have died and gone to Heaven right then and there since I had "seen it all." Little did I know, I really hadn't seen much of anything yet!

In 1994, I heard about and soon met Dr. Dale Sides, President of Liberating Ministries for Christ International (lmci.org). I took his class called, "Signs, Miracles and Wonders" which was later changed to, "Exercising Spiritual Authority." In it, I learned more about ministering healing and deliverance. He also taught about the power of our tongue and Greek words such as, *rhema* (the spoken Word of God). I had recently discovered these things from my own study and from Charles Capps' book, *The Tongue: A Creative Force* (Capps, 1976). It was also at this time I met my friend and future mentor in deliverance, Larry Coker, President of Truth in Love Ministry.

In the spring of 1995, I had a job relocation to Memphis, TN. There I ministered healing whenever I could and saw countless people healed of different things and freed from evil spirits. I was on a roll! I was seeing visions and finding myself in situations only God could do!

In one such situation, I was so excited about the greatness of Luke 10:19, I could hardly sleep (I have a whole chapter on it in my book, *Ekballo: What the Bible Teaches About Every Christian's Authority Over the Evil Spirit Realm* (Hammond, R., 2011.). On a Saturday morning I was sitting at the counter of a Waffle House reading Luke 10:19, in awe of it. A black man was sitting a few seats down who asked, "Whatcha readin'?" I said, "One of the greatest verses in the Bible!" He asked what it was. I told him. He asked why I thought so. I told him. He said. "I'm the pastor of a church. My people need to hear this." The next day, to his surprise, I showed up in his church. Out of the hundreds of people there, everybody knew who the "new person" was because I was the only white man! He said, "Everybody, meet Bob." I waved. "Yesterday, Bob taught me the Bible. Bob, come up here and teach them." So, I did!

Soon after speaking at the church, I was at my prayer spot and I heard the Lord speak to my spirit, "Send your writing to all the churches in Memphis." I had written about what I was learning and experiencing in a thirty page script but hadn't published my book yet. WOW! That's a great idea, I thought. As I pondered it (Don't ponder, do!), I began to talk myself out of it. Who was I to do that? I wasn't a Dr. or reverend or pastor. I hadn't even graduated from Bible college or seminary! Who would care what Bob Hammond wrote? I needed more experience and credentials and so on and so on. Before you knew it, I stopped in my tracks (When God works in you, don't argue with Him...Philippians 2:13-14!). Everything ground to a halt too.

For the next ten years, I fumbled and stumbled. Yes, I still saw some healings and deliverances, but I was not where God wanted me to be. Whenever I tried to pick up my script and continue my writing, I knew it was not the right time; the Spirit would not allow it. During those ten years, my personal and professional life began to fall apart. It was my 50th birthday and after I did a presentation at a sales meeting and they had cake for me, they fired me!

A week or two later, I was in church and the Lord spoke to my spirit, "Do you want to know why you got fired on your 50th birthday?" I said, "Yes," thinking that the devil was after me or some such thing. He said, "For the first 50 years you've been living for yourself. Now it's time to do something for me." I said, "Yes, sir!" God had allowed me get me fired and many other things to get me where I needed to be! I wasn't living a life of sin, but a life for myself and not totally committed to Him.

I wasn't sure what this meant at the time, but a couple of months later I found myself enrolled in Bible College: Great Lakes Christian College in Lansing, Michigan. Two years later I graduated with a Bible Theology degree and a 3.98 GPA (I always wanted to know what it was like to be an A student...you know, one of "them." Well, I did it.).

A few weeks later, I married the best wife in the world! Again, only God could have pulled that off the way He did! She's my biggest fan and frees me up to teach and minister. I don't care what anybody thinks when I'm teaching because she's sitting there with that "You're my man" look!

Before you knew it, I was in seminary at Liberty University (online) and quickly earned my Masters in Biblical Studies. While finishing up my masters, I was at my prayer spot and the Lord said, "It's time to get working on your writing." I had waited thirteen years for the go ahead and now I had it! I told the BWITW (best wife in the world) who said, "You need to publish it as a book." I knew she was right but had no idea how to do it. The Lord filled in the gaps and in early 2011, it was done.

I had lost contact with Larry Coker during my fumble, stumble time but got his phone number and called him in early 2011. Before calling, the BWITW said, "If he invites you to go to India, you need to go." When we spoke, one of the first things Larry did was to invite me to go to India with him. He has a ministry in India and has ministered and traveled there for over twenty years. Well, I went, and went seven more times after that in successive summers. I learned a lot about deliverance from him over the years and had to put out the second edition to my book soon after the first trip due to the many updates I needed to add. Eventually, the third edition was needed and published.

In India, we were part of a team of ministers that did deliverance for large groups of people at one time (up to 200) as well as small groups of about 4. There was great learning from a plethora of experiences. By the end of 2022, I had been a part of, or led about 75 large group deliverances in India and the United States along with numerous small groups. We have helped about 1,000 people get free from evil spirits. After my first experience years earlier, never in my wildest dreams did I think this would ever happen!

We were going under the name of Ekballo Ministry, but my daughter said, "Dad, nobody knows what that means. You need a name they can relate to." So, I came up with about a dozen lame ideas and hers was, by far, the best: Shattered Shackles Ministry. She then gave me a Christmas present of a website and so shatteredshackles.com was formed.

After the first India trip, deliverance opportunities in the United States came frequently and the BWITW joined in. Spur of the moment deliverances occurred and we started to do weekend ones to be more thorough. As word got out, people came from Michigan, New York, the east coast, Arkansas and points in between, as well as our local community. Our team of deliverance ministers has grown to over thirty and invitations to minister deliverance in other states are growing.

We all have a ministry and if we fumble and stumble, like I did, then we will not get results with God. But, if we walk with Him and don't argue with Him when He leads us, we will see Him do exceeding abundantly above all that we could ask or think. And don't forget that He gets all the praise and glory!

Sections

The book is divided into fifteen sections: Demons Speaking Through People, Sex Spirits, Suicide Spirits, False Gods, Rejection Spirits, Witchcraft & The Occult Spirits, Generational Iniquity, Spirits of Infirmity, Casting Demons Out By The Spoken Word of God, Casting Demons Off of People, Individuals Under 20 Years of Age, Haunted Homes, Anger Spirits, Miscellaneous and Minimum Results. Why did I choose these categories? These are common things we run into and, for learning purposes, the reader can get a good idea of what to expect to encounter when doing deliverance.

Yes, I could have included such things as fear, depression, anxiety or trauma, but a line needed to be drawn so as not to have too many or too few. Fifteen allows for almost all of them to have at least 10 and less than 20.

In addition, at the end of each section, all other stories matching the same category but that are in other sections, are noted by number so that if, for example, the reader is interested in seeing more stories that include demons speaking through people, they can find them easily since all the stories are numbered, in order, from 1 through 200.

Chapter 1
Demons Speaking Through People

There are 22 occurrences (33 records) of demons being cast out of people in the Bible. In 8 of those occurrences, demons are specifically recorded speaking through people (Mark 1:24 & Luke 4:34, Luke 4:41, Mark 3:11, Mark 5:7, 9 & 12 & Luke 8:28, 30 & 32, Matthew 8:29 & 31, Mark 9:26, Acts 8:7, Acts 16:17). That is roughly 1 in 3 or 36%. Frank Hammond, in his very popular book, *Pigs in the Parlor* (Hammond, F. 2010), said he observed over the years about 1 in 13 or 8% of the time demons spoke through people. My wife and I estimate about 1 in 2 or 50% per person ministered to.

Why the discrepancy? It may depend on how one defines it; is it per person or per session? Over the course of a weekend, we may only have a demon speak through someone one time out of 10 sessions. So, is that 100% or 10%? In the end, the important thing is that the demon is booted out!

Generally speaking, demons don't want to speak because it will give away their presence. They want to hide. But, when they are exposed through people confessing and repenting of their sins and from their forgiving others who have hurt them, then the spirits are vulnerable and do not have a right to stay any longer. That's when they start to manifest in different ways including speaking through people.

This usually starts with a head shaking back and forth to indicate "No" when they are being commanded out in Jesus' name. When that doesn't throw us off (Don't you wonder why an evil spirit would even think that shaking one's head like that would cause us to stop?), then "No" will frequently be spoken. Then what may come out is, "I won't come out," "I like it here," "I've been here a long time," "Shut up," "Leave me alone," or "Go away." One of my favorites over the years was "I'll come out in 10 minutes."

Don't be surprised by what you might hear. "I'll kill you!" "I hate you!" "Nooo! I see angels coming!" "F*** you!" When demons are called by name, we've heard: Pride: "I am the smartest woman in the world!" Indecision: "Should I come out, or should I stay? I don't know.

What do you think?" Suicide: "I'll kill myself." Murder: "I'll kill you!" Serpent: "Snakes, snakes, snakes." Slumber: "I'm tired." Self hatred: "I'm a bad wife (mother, sister, daughter, husband, father, brother, son, person, etc.)." When asked for the lead spirit in charge of other spirits to give us its name, we've heard, "Fear," "Legion," "Would it surprise you if I said, Satan?" "HATRED!!" "Temper," "Shebaraj [King Serpent]," "White wolf" and others. Like I said, don't be surprised like we were when we heard, "Nice try, but I'm not coming out! Ha-ha!"

Do not converse with evil spirits. They are master manipulators. Jesus gave them two commands, "Shut up" or "Come out and away." He only asked one question, "What is your name?" He did not converse so neither should we.

Oh, and let me not forget to let you know, if you are ministering to and commanding spirits to come out of the person, you may hear a good old fashioned, gut-wrenching, glass breaking, ear drum bursting, neighborhood shaking, eye opening scream that indicates that the demon is about to come out!!

#1...Head Severed

My name is Teresa Jones.

At the time of my deliverance, I was living 3 hours away from the church in which it took place. I had attended this church regularly for several years back and occasionally over the other years. I make that point because I believe it was important for MY deliverance to feel comfortable in the environment.

My best friend had become involved in the ministry of deliverance and she had gone through her own deliverance a few months prior, and felt I would benefit from it. I had been successful in my professional life throughout the years; however, my personal life was a hot mess. I had known for years there was a veil between my professional success and my personal life, and didn't understand how or why. I was ready to get rid of whatever was causing me to destroy my personal life.

I traveled to Bowling Green two weeks prior to my deliverance to attend the Deliverance Bible study lead by Bob Hammond, which was created for persons who had either gone through deliverance, were deliverance team members or persons who were interested in going through deliverance. I sat and absorbed every second of the night. I knew it was something I wanted to do – needed to do! I was so tired of being sick and tired all of my life. At the end of the study, Bob offered to lend me a copy of his book, *Ekballo: What the Bible Teaches About Every Christian's Authority Over the Evil Spirit Realm*, to read but I had to promise to bring it back. I promised I would and I did.

I became a Christian and was baptized when I was 11 or 12. I've attended church over the years but not Sunday school very often. I found it to be boring for several reasons. 1. The Bible was difficult to read and understand. This played out differently after my deliverance. 2. I never felt the Sunday school teacher could explain the study in the manner I needed. More times than not, I would ask a question and they couldn't give me an answer. 3. I didn't want the superficial stuff. I wanted and hungered for the "meat and potatoes" of the Bible and Jesus. I wasn't getting it and couldn't seem to find it. This would change after my deliverance.

I decided on my way home after the Deliverance Bible Study that I was going to do everything I could to empower myself with the help of Jesus Christ to overcome whatever it was on the other side of that veil that I had been fighting my whole life. I was determined I was going to be prepared and I was going to win in the name of Jesus. I decided to fast from the TV. I knew watching TV was my escape. So for the next two weeks, every time I wanted to watch TV, I would read Bob's book. And boy, did it blow me away. Everything started to make sense. Finally, "meat and potatoes." I consumed the book, cover to cover. I prayed multiple times a day, every day. I researched taking communion on my own and took it once a week for the two weeks prior to my deliverance. I didn't know it then, but everything I was doing was going to pack a powerful punch to my demons.

Deliverance weekend arrived. During my trip to Bowling Green Friday afternoon, I was feeling some anxiety that I passed off as natural nervousness of the unknown. The closer I got to Bowling Green, the more anxious I became. My heart was pounding. It felt like I couldn't breathe. My thoughts were racing. Was I going to have a panic attack? Is this a heart attack?

Should I pull over to the side of the interstate? Maybe I shouldn't do this? What if something happens to me while I'm there? So I prayed – dear Jesus - help me get there. I later learned this was a ploy by the demons to keep me from going.

Deliverance started Friday night with a short fellowship of food/

drink and meeting the participants and deliverance team members. I was still feeling some anxiety but was determined to go through with it. I noticed I yawned several times and passed it off as just being tired. After all, it was Friday, I had worked all week and the 3 hour drive made me even more tired. I learned later there was more to the yawning than I realized.

We started deliverance early Saturday morning, kicking the day off with biblical readings and teachings. There were 6 – 1 hour sessions that followed on Saturday and 3 sessions on Sunday. Each session addressed different possible strongholds and each resulted in different manifestations of my demons. Demons aren't always what society tells us they are or look like but can manifest as other "things."

At the beginning of each session, I was given a list of strongholds that were used to prompt memories of acts of sin, people who hurt me, people I had hurt (physically, mentally, emotionally and sexually). I cannot say this emphatically enough. It is imperative you be honest about EVERYTHING. I knew in my soul that my team members were not there to judge me but to help set me free from my torments, my demons, and demons will not leave unless they are called out and commanded to leave in the name of Jesus. So, if you don't confess, that demon will remain. My team members were Karen – who is Bob's wife, Tina and Shelby. Bob assisted from time to time in later sessions.

First session: I completed the questionnaire. I was asked to repeat a prayer spoken by Karen. I was sitting at a round table: Karen to my left, then Tina and Shelby to my right. It is by habit that when I pray I close my eyes as I did this time. I was sitting close to the table with my arms stretched out in front of me with my hands clasped together. This sounds trivial but again I've since learned its importance. I started repeating the prayer. I was strong in voice but noticed the longer it went the more difficult it was to talk. Immediately, after the prayer stopped, my arms, hands and wrists started feeling funny, like they hurt. Seconds after the prayer stopped, my head bowed to the table and I let out a scream that was not me. My arms and hands were stretched out in front of me and they started banging on the table while I was screaming. This went on for several seconds/minutes then my arms stopped banging and only my hands were beating on the table. I was aware of every moment yet I thought I had no control over my body.

As soon as the demon manifested, the team members went to work. Often demons will manifest in different parts of your body so they were asking me if I was feeling discomfort anywhere. It's hard to explain the feeling but it was in my back, between my shoulder blades and in my spine. Tina came to my rescue and began rubbing my spine and back area while demanding the demon to come out. At some point my head was hurting pretty bad. They were telling the demon to come out in the name of Jesus. This continued for a bit and the session ended with no real result. However, I knew in my soul that the quickness of the demon manifesting was due to my preparation the prior two weeks. The demons were stirred up because they knew my Jesus was coming after them.

Second session: I completed a different questionnaire and sat with my arms folded across my chest resting on the table. As the sessions continued each time, I would say the prayer, starting with a strong voice and head held high. But as the prayer proceeded, my head would gradually drop, my voice would get lower, and it became more and more difficult to repeat the prayer. Karen would command the demon to let me speak and it would get better. The demons clearly had control over my voice and at times I felt I couldn't breathe. Again, Karen would command the demons to let me breathe, and it would get better. The manifestations all started during the prayer but with different manifestations after that.

With my arms folded, my left arm was laying on my right arm. My left hand started patting my right arm in a strange, unnatural manner. This lead into my arms and hands and wrists feeling strange again and especially my wrists. I had the uncontrollable need to "wring my wrist." Shortly after that began, I started raising my arms in a twisting manner while wringing my wrist.

The team members were commanding the demons to come out. Karen was touching my left shoulder and arm, Tina was rubbing my back and Shelby was rubbing my right arm. The demons decided they didn't like that. I started telling them to "stop touching me," "leave me alone," "go away," "No, No, No," and twisting in my chair trying to get away from them. By this time, I was crying and slobbering. Karen was trying to wipe my nose and mouth. My hair was messed up and in my face. I turned to Karen and heard in my head, "Tell her you want to hurt her." I knew it wasn't from me and was from the demon. I wanted to tell her to run but I couldn't speak. I was aware of everything but had no control, or so I thought. I was finally able to tell her the demon wanted to hurt her in which she stated, "I'm not afraid of you. You can't hurt me." She asked the demon, "Who are you? What is your name?" And I couldn't answer other than saying it started with a "B." We never knew for sure the name of the demon.

About that time Bob came into the room, which he does often during deliverances to see how everything is going. He sat down beside Karen and immediately began talking to me. I was looking at him thru slanted eyes which I knew were not my own. He asked "Who are you?" I would only shake my head no. He started naming demons and when he said demon of mockery, I started laughing. And the demon said "I'm not going anywhere. I've been here for a long time." The casting out continued. There was coughing and spitting in each of the sessions.

I don't know the procession of the next manifestation in terms of which sessions. I only have memories of the order of manifestations.

The demons kept coming back each session. I was being told each time to fight them. Tell them they had to leave in the name of Jesus Christ and that they could no longer live inside of me. They were no longer wanted and did not have a strong hold on me. I had a hard time with this. I understood the concept but you have to find the strength and courage, and most of all faith that you can do it – to know Jesus is there to help you – to cast the demons out in Jesus name.

Sunday.

Bob started coming into the room to help during each session if needed. Looking back, I laugh each time I think of this because let me tell you, those demons did not like Bob and wanted no part of him. Bob is a man of great faith and knows the teachings of Jesus. When Bob entered the room, the demons' eyes were focused on him and no one else mattered.

Another session: Bob came into the room and sat down. He stated he was going to help the team and asked if I was OK with him touching me. I knew it was a matter of respect for a man to ask to touch a woman, plus the demons didn't want the other team members touching me. At each session, it was becoming more and more difficult to speak during the prayer. The manifestation began and I started wringing my wrist, twisting my arms and by this time had graduated to twisting my body in my chair. Bob came over and sat beside me. Immediately, no one existed in the room but Bob. My back was to Karen. He took hold of my wrist because I began pushing on him and telling him to go away and to leave me alone. Remember when you were a kid and your sibling would hold you down and you couldn't get up? And there was no way you were going to get that person off you because they were bigger and stronger than you? That's exactly the feeling I had. The demon couldn't get away from Bob and it didn't want to surrender.

Things calmed down some, Bob let go of me and I had the urge to bend down toward the floor. I was taking my arms and scratching the floor but in my mind's eye it was sand. The demon wanted me to get on the floor and writher around. My voice in my head rose up and said no!

I knew at that moment I had the power to overcome the demon. I sat back up in the chair and a few minutes later, it happened again. This time I commanded the demon to be cast out in the name of Jesus and to never return. Then I saw in my mind's eye the demon come out. It looked like a big centipede with a worm like body and long tentacles on each side. This time it slithered away on the sand, without me. What a relief!! But, little did I know, it wasn't over yet.

Bob and the team members knew there was still a demon or demons in there because of some of the same minor manifestations. My hand would slap the table, my leg would jingle up and down, the look in my eye and how I would talk.

Last session: We brainstormed some more trying to figure out what could be the stronghold. I remembered I had attended a service at a Hindu Temple in Nashville many years ago for a Religion class for extra credit. The session began and I literally could barely speak the words of the prayer. The prayer ended and we went after that demon. I truly believed now that by the power of Jesus Christ, coupled with my courage, we could cast the demon out.

The calling out of the demon began. It was intense and lasted for a long time. I remember Bob coming into the room and sitting across the table from me, just observing me, not saying a word. I was sitting down at the time. I just felt abnormal. I was looking at him but not through my eyes. Shortly thereafter, I was up on my feet, literally screaming telling the demon to leave me in the name of Jesus Christ. It did not belong there, it was not wanted, and it had to leave. I commanded it to leave by the power given to me by Jesus Christ! All of a sudden, in my mind's eye, I saw a serpent, with a jewel behind its left eye, leaving my body, slithering across the table and in a flash, I took my hand (hitting the table) and chopped its head off!..... It was over.

My life has changed so much since my deliverance. People tell me they see a physical change in me and I feel it. I smile, laugh and enjoy life so much more now. I'm a different person and I embrace that every day. I can now read the Bible and understand what GOD is telling me. Before it was just all words without much meaning. It makes sense now and I know the demons were not letting me understand it. I have had back issues for years in my spine. Since my deliverance, that issue has diminished tremendously. It has been suggested that a family of baby serpents could have been living in my spine area and left with the coughs and spitting.

I give praise to my Lord and Savior, Jesus Christ, for giving his followers the power to cast out demons in his name. I'm so grateful for Bob and Karen Hammond for following GOD's command to create and follow through with the Deliverance Ministry, and to my other team members.

Blessings!

#2...I'm Gonna Break Your F------ Neck!

On a cool fall afternoon in 1979, a few friends and I were witnessing to people in a park in Parkersburg, West Virginia. As the leaves gently descended from their trees to the ground below we struck up a conversation with a young man who was about our age, the early twenties, and told him about Jesus Christ. I wish I could say that I was on top of the situation and in deep concern for this man, but the truth is that I was not "into it" that day and wished I was somewhere else. That all changed in an instant!

As we continued to speak to this young man he started acting "funny." One of my friends looked at me and said, "This guy is weird!" Moments later the man looked directly at me with his eyes piercing a canyon sized hole through me and said in a ***different voice*** and with complete sincerity and no doubt saying what he meant, "***I'm gonna break your f------ neck!***" Huh?! What?! You're gonna do what?! Ummmmmmm. Now what do I do? They didn't teach me about this in church! I knew what it was that was speaking to me: a demon. That much I knew but now what? Negotiate?! Call fire down from Heaven?! Pray?! Run?! My mind was in a tizzy as I froze in my tracks. Somehow or other the "conversation" ended and we parted ways. I was glad I would not have to deal with him again! I would much rather run across a nice person who just says, "Yes" to Jesus and stay away from those possessed ones. Boy, was I relieved!

The next night, ***he showed up in church***!

We were part of a home church with about twenty-five to thirty who attended. Here, I thought, he wouldn't dare to misbehave! Certainly all of these Christians together would somehow have a calming effect on him. Maybe he would be that nice person and accept Jesus so that all of his troubles would go away! We could rejoice together and praise and worship and, "***F--- you!***" he said to the person to his left, "***F--- you!***" he said to the person on his right!! The leader, who knew I had met him in the park, said to me, "Get him out of here! He's possessed!" Oh, now that was all I needed! The guy who wants to break my f------ neck has come to make good on his promise and I'm supposed to escort him outside *alone*! Visions of scenes from *The Exorcist* ran through my mind and I could see my head twisting like a pretzel before falling off.

But with fear and trembling I obeyed, thinking that if he got one blow in I could escape and go get help or if I was going to meet Jesus sooner than expected, that would not be all bad. As we went outside together, I maintained a safe distance of a few feet. He was mumbling while looking up at the moon, tapping one foot on the ground continuously and jerking around slightly. He complained that his "ears were burning." I asked him why and he said, "He's doing it." I said, "Who?" He replied, "Billy Bad-ass." He had a demon named Billy Bad-ass. At least I knew the name of my executioner! I asked him if he had any other "friends" that did things to him and he answered in the affirmative but that he could not tell me their names. I asked him why he couldn't tell me their names (By now I was trembling more than he was!). His answer sent chills through me as he finally looked at me, not in an evil way, but more like one that was pleading for help, "Because I'll die."

My attitude changed. I wanted to help. I had learned about the "power of God" and how it is stronger than any demon but I did not know how to use it. I knew that nobody inside knew how to either. My theology was crumbling because I was face to face with someone who truly needed help, who did not come to kill me, but came for help because we had told him we could give it to him. Unknowingly, ***we had lied to him***. Not only did we not help him, we kicked him out! We were just another dead end road in his search for relief.

Shortly after this, he left and I have never seen him again. As I watched him walk away, still mumbling and looking up at the moon and trying to relieve his burning ears, I felt terrible. We had failed him…***I had failed him***. But at the same time I became determined to know what to do and began a search of the Scriptures, the Bible, to find out just what we are to do in these situations. Since that day, similar situations have come up and because of the road the Lord led me down and how He taught me, I have been able to help demonized people get deliverance (over 1,000) and receive Jesus Christ as their Lord.

#3…A Vision Of Jesus

This deliverance is one that you could never forget because Jesus himself showed up in a vision!

When we finish a deliverance session in India, I usually look around to be sure nobody is still manifesting and if they are, I go to see if I can help while the others are enjoying a 15 minute tea break. Evangeline still needed help as Beaula (speaks English) and Sajina (doesn't speak English), team members, were ministering to her. I watched and slowly got involved as the opportunity came to me. Evangeline was manifesting a defiant spirit, then a mocking spirit and then a fear spirit. The three of us talked among ourselves to see what to do about it and how to minister to her.

Eventually, the tea break ended and the next teaching started so I suggested we take Evangeline to the vacant room in the back and continue. When we did, we looked for roots of entry to "cut" and commanded the spirits out. As we did this, I could tell the demon speaking through her was mad (Wouldn't you be mad if you were a demon being cast out?), but as I continued to command the spirit out, Beaula and Sajini stopped speaking, so I did too. But, the angry words kept coming out!

I asked Beaula, "What is going on?" She said that Evangeline and the evil spirit were arguing through her mouth! Sometimes the demon would speak and say something like, "I am not coming out! I've been here a long time and I'm staying!" Then Evangeline would say something like, "No! You have to go! Jesus is my Lord now and you must leave!" This "fight" went on for about a minute and then Evangeline started jumping and clapping and praising God! She danced and was full of excitement! The strongman spirit had left with his friends! The three of us were crying with joy as well!

Suddenly, Evangeline stared into the corner and was marveling at something with amazement while she slowly walked toward the corner! I looked over there and saw nothing. I asked Beaula what was happening and she said that Evangeline was seeing Jesus and He was glorious and magnificent and so on and so on! He was looking at her with loving eyes, etc.! I have had angels make their presence known before, but not Jesus! Jesus set this captive free!

One thing I took away from this deliverance is the need of the person being delivered to want it...badly...energetically...with a dogged determination! Evangeline would not quit until she won!

#4...She's My Daughter

Rose Marie was 18 years old. About six months earlier, her dad had died. Thankfully, he was saved shortly before he died, but he had lived a tormented life and had treated his family poorly. He kicked Rose Marie, her mom and her siblings out of the house when they became Christians. Even still, his death was a traumatic event for her and because of this, a familiar spirit from him had entered into her. It tormented her with thoughts of her dad and was trying to convince her that *it* was her dad!

About a year earlier, after hearing about how her dad never gave her treats or did anything nice for her, I asked her if I could be her "daddy." She agreed! So, I made it a point to provide treats for her even when I wasn't near her and I have stayed in contact with her.

As we ministered to her, I held on to her and said, "I love you. You're my daughter. Let it go." After I said this a few times, the familiar spirit yelled out of her mouth, "Noooooo! She's *my* daughter!" Shortly after this, the demon left and she has not been tormented again! God be praised!

One interesting side note is that India was formerly a British colony, so English is sort of the universal language of India, but common folk don't speak it. Rose Marie does not speak English, but when the demon spoke English through her, it did so with a British accent!

#5...We Like It Here

I was teaching a Bible study, in our church, with about 15 people in attendance. The topic was deliverance and I showed videos I had taken in India of demonized people being delivered. Sam didn't appreciate it. In fact, he caused a disturbance in the middle of Bible study insisting that this doesn't happen in America and that Christians can't have demons anyway. Well, I guess you know, we didn't agree!

About three months later, he contacted me because his sister, Rita, a long time Christian, had serious problems. He said, "It has to be the devil." My wife and I met with him and another believer to minister deliverance to her. Imagine that!

Rita was unable to eat. The "voices" had convinced her that she needed to fast...all the time. If she ate, they said, she would go to Hell. So, she stopped eating. She lost 50 lbs. and was taken to the hospital and put on an IV so she wouldn't die (She didn't have 50 lbs to lose!).

This is when Sam brought her to us, just skin and bones. She really didn't come enthusiastically, but still, she wanted help. She had a secret sin and the voices told her that if she revealed it, they would kill her. This scared her, but ultimately, she knew she was going to die anyway, so now or later really didn't matter. Dying now meant she wouldn't starve to death. So, she revealed her secret sin and repented of it. Of course, this was the key to deliverance from the evil spirits.

As we commanded the spirits out, Sam could feel them going up her spine as he had his hand on her back. They slowly moved up and as they got closer to the top, they started speaking, "We're not coming out! We like it here!" and so on. When they got to the top of her back, she coughed violently and out they came! She was free! Praise the Lord!

Sam, who was disruptive three months earlier and just knew that Christians couldn't have demons, said, "I've never seen anything like this before!" Need I say that Sam now knows that Christians can have demons?

Several months later, Rita came to see us. She had gained all the weight back and was her normal self! Jesus does come to set the captives free!

#6...F*** You!

We sometimes get surprised when we do deliverance. We are not shocked, because, in a way, we expect surprises. The weekend deliverance we were doing on Carla was moving along smoothly with no wild manifestations, but it had a surprise near the end.

Apparently one demon was getting upset and coming to the surface without us noticing because when we least expected it, it screamed, "F*** you!" I think Carla was as surprised as we were! We asked her where that came from and she told us that when she was younger, she used to say it a lot, almost like a game. Then it became a habit and sort of an idol to her which is what allowed the demon to come in. She found herself saying it when she was mad at people.

She confessed her sin of cussing like this and we commanded

the "F*** you" spirit to come out. When it did, do I have to tell you what it was saying?! I think not! God be praised!

#7...Legion

During a three day women's conference held at a local church in Mexico City, I was translating for a pastor's wife, while in a small breakout session, with about forty women in attendance.

We were sharing how women's wounds sometimes run deep causing them to be bitter or not having freedom in their lives. It wasn't intended to be a session for deliverance but just about freedom in your emotions and dealing with things that women oftentimes hold on to.

A lady, named Olga, was there. She had been invited by one of her friends. She had never given her life to Christ. Being Catholic, she knew about Jesus, but had never made a decision to make Him her Lord. She had knowledge about who Jesus was, but only from a religious perspective. The pastor's wife, Lenoir, was speaking about freedom and allowing God to heal those hurts from their past. It wasn't too long into the session, twenty to thirty minutes into an hour session, and Olga started to manifest in her seat. She kind of growled and grunted. So, we approached her, and I began translating what was coming out of Olga. Olga was bent over in her chair, crying, and snarling a little bit but not anything too big. Ms. Lenoir approached her and started to pray for her and declared Jesus and prayed freedom in Christ over her.

The demon started speaking back. Ms. Lenoir said in English, with me translating, "I command you to come out of her in the name of Jesus." The response was, "No, we won't." Ms. Lenoir said my eyes got as big as dollar coins and asked, "What did they say?" "They said, 'No, we won't'". She responded, "Oh yes you will in the name of Jesus." For some reason Ms. Lenoir asked the demon, "What is your name?" The demon said, in a big deep snarly voice, "We are legion!"

Ms. Lenoir began to take authority over Legion and called them out and commanded that Olga be freed. It wasn't more than five or ten minutes and she was definitely a very different person. The look on her face and how wrinkled and aged she had looked when we first met her was gone and for the rest of the conference she looked younger and more beautiful instead of ragged like earlier. She was beautiful before she got delivered, but after she got delivered, she had grace and peace and youthfulness that came over her.

After she was delivered, Ms. Lenoir directly led her through the sinner's prayer and she received Christ as her Lord and Savior and she came to the rest of the conference, sat in the front row and talked about how much peace she had.

She ended up bringing her son to a couple of the open sessions so he could enjoy the presence of the Lord.

Over the next ten years, I saw her many more times during my visits to the church in Mexico City. She had such a good demeanor and served at the church. She became such an integral part of the helps ministry at the church and even helped other women get freed from demonic oppression and possession.

The hurts and abuse that she endured from the relationship she had with her son's father and the bitterness she had held on to opened the door for her to be possessed.

After encountering Jesus, she was set free and able to give her life to Him. After doing so, she experienced freedom from demonic possession for as long as I knew her after that point.

#8…Lying Tongue

I was on the team in the Transformation class and was assigned to shadow Pastor Britt, one of the great deliverance ministers in India. As we went from person to person, I was gleaning knowledge and wisdom from him. We had come to the last day of the two-week class and I was looking forward to helping Mahesh. He and I had "clicked" since the first day but he had a stubborn spirit that would not come out. It would cause him to stiffen like a board, cause his eyes to get super wide and when I commanded spirits out, it just shook his head, no, and stayed. It would also cause his tongue to go out of his mouth and wiggle around. I thought it must be some kind of sex spirit, but he had confessed all his sex sins including homosexual practices. I was looking forward to assisting Pastor Britt in ministering to Mahesh and seeing the Lord set him free!

I soon became frustrated as the clock was ticking and Pastor Britt was helping someone else when we had agreed to minister to Mahesh. Finally, I said (or thought…I don't remember), "Well Lord, I guess it's just you and me!" Sooner or later, if we are going to walk in the power to God, we need to take the training wheels off, take a deep breath and do it. Somehow we can forget that He is with us and helping us the whole time.

I began to minister to him, like we had before, with his other three mini-team members, and the same thing happened like it had previously...stiffen, buggy eyes, head shake no and tongue waggle. As I looked at him and pondered what to do ***differently***, Mahesh said with a smile, "I'm OK the way I am." Huh?! We've been wrestling with this thing for ten days and he keeps saying he wants to be free and suddenly he's OK the way he is? Then, again with a smile, he said, "Why don't you people leave me alone?" Something is really not right! Other brighter crayons in the box would have caught on sooner, but then I said, "Who am I talking to?" All I got was a smile so I repeated the question and again, I got a smile. I asked five times and got only smiles back. Then Mahesh said, "Brother, I heard you asking me who you are talking to." I replied, "Yes, but the demon wouldn't let you answer me."

Then Mahesh started to cry and repent. He repented for lying to friends about needing money to pay bills and instead using the money to buy booze. He told the Lord how sorry he was for dishonoring Him with his behavior and for lying. He took full blame for his condition instead of blaming his wife for her actions. I knew in my heart of hearts that we were about to have a breakthrough!

When he finished, we commanded the spirits out in the name of Jesus Christ and within thirty seconds they were gone through powerful coughing! He was full of joy and had a new attitude and commitment. I was thankful to the Lord for seeing us through and for helping me take the training wheels off! Most of all, Mahesh was set free by Jesus!

When a deliverance session is over, you frequently can see what happened and why it happened although while it's happening, you don't know. You also see how the Lord was working with you. Mahesh had been saying that he was having trouble forgiving his wife for things she had done when what he really needed to do was repent. The demon spoke English to me because I was one of the leaders of the class and since Mahesh was an English teacher and fluent in English, I wouldn't know it was the demon speaking (None of the mini-team members spoke English.). The others were looking to me for leadership so if it could throw me off, it would throw the others off too. The demon was a lying spirit. It lied by saying, "I'm OK the way I am." and Mahesh had gotten it by continuing to lie to his family and friends; when lying became an idol to him, the spirit had a right to enter. The wagging tongue was a "lying tongue" that Proverbs speaks about. The tongue actually lies because the spirit is in it. By repenting of his lying, Mahesh could then be set free. Without repenting, he would not have gotten rid of it.

#9...I Hate You!

It was the first group deliverance session in the Transformation class and a demon was screaming something, in an Indian language, over and over again, through a lady near the front. Then she looked at me, "I hate you! I hate you! I hate you..." When it was over, I asked the lady, who spoke English, "You have a demon named I Hate You. How did you get it?" "When I was 16, I had a fight with my mother and I said, 'I hate you!' and I've been saying it ever since whenever I get into a fight."

She confessed her sin of dishonoring her mother and cursing her, along with anyone else, and cut any ungodly soul ties and we cast the spirit out of her. For the rest of the class she was adamant about confessing sins and getting "junk" (spirits) out! To God be the glory!

#10...Screams And Thrashing

A significant casting out of demons occurred in the Healing Rooms as a brother brought his sister in for prayer for a severe migraine headache. She had visited the ER that day but still had no relief even with medication! She was in her early sixties and her brother was explaining how she had been saved for about 3 years and was going to church and involved with different groups in her church. Before that, she had held a professional job, had a home and had lost everything due to an addiction to drugs. Her siblings called for an intervention and got her into a rehab program and she had been freed from the addiction for over 3 years but now had these horrible headaches.

As we began to pray over her, I felt led to call out a spirit of condemnation to come out of her. She began to scream and thrash about calling herself stupid and other names for the years that had been wasted. At one point, we had to protect her from hurting herself because she (the demon) was trying to bang her head on the floor. She was crying and saying, "Why did I let drugs ruin my life for so long?!" When she said this, we commanded a spirit of self hatred and condemnation to come out which they did! She began to be at peace at which point we were able to minister the love and forgiveness of God to her. Her migraine subsided and her brother reported a few months later that his sister had made a tremendous change and joy had returned to her life! Praise be to

God! He heals the broken-hearted and sets the captives free!!

#11…I'm Leaving!

We were in the Transformation class in India. Suddenly, without warning, a demon in a woman in the back screamed out in the Tamil language, "*I came here to disrupt this meeting! I can't do it! I'm leaving!*" The demon ended up leaving the meeting a day or two later… without the woman. Glory to God!

#12…Noooo! Angels Are Coming!

I don't know the lady's name or what the spirits were that were in her. But during the teachings she sat in the front row and was very prim and proper...very lady-like! But when the evil spirits manifested in her, she was flat on her back with her arms and legs flailing away and she was screaming over and over, "*Nooooo! I see angels coming!*"

That poor demon (not really!)! The sight of angels, which exceed in strength, coming to drag it away was just too much to bear! It must be awful to be a puny demon...but wonderful to be someone Jesus has set free from them!

#13…Screamin' Demon

I was working for a large company and it had a cafeteria where workers could eat lunch if they wanted to. One day, the very moment I walked through the door to the cafeteria, a woman, named Aye Aye, screamed. It was the type of scream I had heard before: demonic. Hundreds of people who had been talking away suddenly stopped and there was dead silence. Maybe 30 seconds later, she screamed again. Someone in management took her to the office.

I knew her; she was from the Far East and was Buddhist. I went over to where she had been sitting and one of them said, "She has an evil spirit." I knew that and I thought about how people who practice false religions know more about demons than Christians do who don't know that they have authority over them.

I went to the office to check on her and one of the managers that I knew well was with her. He had been a missionary in India for three years and knew a lot about demons. She was sort of in a daze and not aware of her surroundings. I said to him, "Should I try something?" He nodded yes. I said, "She might scream again," and he nodded again.

Since there were others close by, I whispered into her ear, "Come out in the name of Jesus." and she coughed them out violently, yet relatively quietly too.

About three months later, Aye Aye came to church with us and got saved right there! She ended up bringing other friends of hers to church and continued in the Christian walk. The screamin' demon never returned. God be praised!

I wondered if it was just a coincidence that the demon screamed when I came into the cafeteria or if my presence had something to do with it. Shortly after the incident, I heard a deliverance minister say during a teaching, "It is an awesome thing when demons scream when you walk into a room." That was my answer and it impressed upon me that a believer, who has Christ in him, does affect the spiritual surroundings!

#14...See If You Can Cast Me Out!

I was in the Transformation class in India and during the praise and worship, a demon in a man in the front started yelling at the leader as he led the songs! It was an angry yell. The leader just kept on going as if nothing was happening.

Later, I asked him what the demon was saying. He said, "My friends are leaving because of the praising, but see if you can cast me out!" The one speaking was obviously a more powerful "boss" demon that later did come out.

One thing that impressed me was how much control a demonized person has over his own self. Even though he was severely demonized, he sat in the front in order to be close to the Word of God and the praise and worship. Had the "boss" been in total control, it never would have allowed the man to be there.

#15...Low Demonic Voice

My name is Brenda Cruey.

When I came in to this group, I was skeptical of the whole thing. Wasn't sure it wasn't an occult.

In December, 2020, Andy stood in my kitchen and said, "Mom Brenda, you can speak in a very low voice [implying a demonic voice]." I said, "I know and I have before," and I kinda blew it off.

I blew Andy off several times! After coming for deliverance, I know why Andy's eyes shine like diamonds.

I cannot thank y'all (as a whole) for what wonderful and <u>much needed freedom</u> I received this Freedom Weekend!

#16…What Are You Trying To Do To Her?

I was continuously being driven to do acts of sin and constantly beating myself up and feeling remorseful about it. I reached out to Matt who was the pastor that baptized me when I received salvation and he mentioned that in all my years of talking to him he was thinking it may be something demonic holding me. He gave me Bob's number and I reached out.

I also was dating a girl who had manifested a demon one night when I spoke to her about Christ. She was speaking about how she didn't like going to sleep in the dark and always left the bathroom light on. Her previous roommates used to make fun of her and when she came back to bed we went to sleep. I couldn't sleep and a couple minutes later she turned to me with the coldest eyes I had ever seen and an energy that frightened me. She said, "What are you trying to do?" I said, "Go to sleep, obviously." Then she said, "What are you trying to do to her?" and turned over again. I was freaked out so I got up, turned the light on and woke her up. She had no recollection of what I told her had happened. She asked, "Are you going to leave?" I said, "No, not if you pray with me." We prayed against the spirit in the name of Christ and went to sleep.

Soon after, I called Bob and discussed going to Kentucky over the phone. He said he would like to speak with my girlfriend as well after I told him the story and I arranged a call. When we called Bob she had no issues but once we got on the phone with him the spirit in her started getting restless. After the call she mocked Bob and his wife and said nasty things which seemed totally out of line for the loving conversation we had on the phone. The next day she called me and was crying. She said that she wouldn't go, told her mother about it and they decided it was fanatical and she said if I went by myself we would be through.

I went anyway and Bob was very hospitable and let me stay over. We went through a variety of sins to ask forgiveness for and then would do casting out sessions. I threw up a pink liquid on the rejection spirit casting and felt choking in my throat for another one to be cast out that I don't remember specifics for. I had tears and felt a great deal of relief after all was said and done.

After everything, during the ministry of the Holy Spirit session, music was played and candles lit just to bask in God's presence and ask Him to reveal anything else we needed to know. I saw a bull statue in a green mist which I still don't understand what it meant.

Since the weekend I have found myself sometimes as a dog to vomit and felt the oppression occur again. When it happens, I take authority and cast out spirits in the bathroom myself and it gives me relief. I am not entirely free at this point but I can't deny the reality of what occurred. I am thankful for Bob equipping me with the knowledge of how these spirits work and equipping me with warfare strategies.

#17…Many Spirits

A lady had walked a long way to come to a meeting at our Church. During the teaching, I had noticed she was talking to herself. I then sent someone to check on her. She continued talking to herself, off and on, throughout the teaching.

After I talked some with her, she said she had a headache. I asked if I could pray for her and she said, "Yes." So I began praying. I said, "I rebuke you, headache, in the Name of Jesus." She began thrusting herself up and down in the chair and I knew it was not her but evil spirits. I continued to pray as the Holy Spirit led me. I said, "Depression, anxiety and anything not of God, come out now in Jesus' name." She was still being thrust up and down in the chair. I continued praying for her and laying my hands on her head. She began spitting out the evil spirits in a trash can. So I heard in my spirit, "Tell them to tell you who they are." So I asked, "Who are you in Jesus' name?" The demon said, "Lucifer" in a scary voice! I said, "Lucifer, come out in Jesus' name!" She spit it out! I said, "Who else is in there?" The demon said, "Serpent" and another said, "Python" and another said, "Leviathan" and I commanded them out and she spit them out!

I asked how she was doing and she said she was okay. I kept her hair out of her face and my hands still on her head. I said, "Who else is in there?" The lady said, "I am not for sure." And she began explaining perhaps a mermaid. I told the lady, "Say, 'Mermaid spirit, come out in Jesus' name!'" She did and she spit it out.

These all came out screaming before she spit them out! Then

when I asked who the chief demon was it began speaking in a foreign language to me. I could sense it was not a Holy Spirit prayer language. I told the demon to shut up and come out in Jesus' name! She spit it out.

During all this there were two other people in the room with us. One person was praying silently and the other was praying in their prayer language. I asked the lady how she was doing and she said that she felt better. To God be the glory. Thank you, Jesus.

For more stories that include demons talking through people, see #'s 21, 34, 35, 36, 40, 42, 43, 47, 49, 51, 69, 70, 72, 88, 111, 116, 117, 119, 159, 172, 175, 193.

Chapter 2
Sex Spirits

Probably 90% of the time, or more, when we minister to someone, sex spirits are present. Sin is idolatry (Colossians 3:5) and sex outside of marriage is sin. One should flee from sexual immorality (1 Corinthians 10:14) otherwise he is fellowshipping with demons (1 Corinthians 10:14). Furthermore, when one fornicates (sex outside of marriage) he sins against himself (1 Corinthians 6:18). One of the best ways to invite demons into yourself is to have sex outside the context of a committed marital relationship; in any other way, you are exposing yourself to demonization.

God is not old fashioned when it comes to sex. It is understood in the medical community, that when two people have sex, there is a physical change in their bodies that affects their thought processes and future decisions. Having multiple sex partners limits an individual's ability to have healthy bonding within marriage (McIilhaney & McKissic Bush, 2008). I'll spare you the scientific terms and physiological explanations, but in Genesis 2:24, when God says, "…the two shall become one flesh," He knew what he was talking about! It is literally true. Having one sex partner for life is God's plan and appropriately so. Understanding how bonding through sex occurs helps explain why women will remain in abusive and violent relationships. She says, "But I love him," which is probably true, but the reality is that she is bonded to him; therefore it's too painful to let him go. God knew what He was doing when He set this up, we should humble ourselves and obey.

This bonding is called a "soul-tie." When sex is abused, multiple soul-ties occur and demons can ride on these and be transferred through sexual contact. A person who has sinned sexually, may suddenly have homosexual desires that he/she never had before. This is probably due to these spirits being transferred through different people and ending up in him/her. The sins must be confessed and repented of and ungodly soul-ties severed. Furthermore, sex spirits can then drive the person to continue to commit fornication, even against his/her will (2 Timothy 2:26). Be sure your soul-ties are godly ones.

#18...Grandma's Prayers

After Kevin would finish, I would go into the bathroom to clean up. Something didn't seem right. I looked up to him and trusted him; he was 13 and I was 8. What does an 8-year-old girl know about anything anyway? But I was confused. It went on for two years and sometime later I realized that my brother had sexually molested me.

Sexual promiscuity is common among teenage girls who have been molested. I was no exception. I had sex with a boy for the first time when I was in 8th grade; he was 19. In high school I had sex with a lot of boys and girls starting in 9th grade. I was an athlete and was on several teams. About half the girls on the teams were having sex with other girls so it seemed natural to do the same, plus it was a new school for me and I wanted to fit in. I even had sex with one of my female teachers for about 6 months. Had anyone found out, she not only would have been fired, but would have gone to prison.

We lived in Morgantown, WV, and Grandma Simpson lived nearby. She was the one person I trusted; she was always there for me. By the time I graduated in 2011, she had found out that I was living a gay lifestyle. She prayed daily for me that I would become revolted by my lifestyle and would come to Jesus.

By the time I entered West Virginia University, I was full into being a lesbian. I got a girlfriend, Jamie, who was also entering WVU so we became roommates. This went on for two years and it was toxic. We hurt each other with our words and actions and then we broke up. Jamie took it so hard that she attempted suicide by hanging. She would have succeeded except that the metal rod the rope was attached to broke.

Grandma Simpson kept praying for me to become revolted and find Jesus.

I met Penelope online and we hit it off. She was from California so I moved there to be with her. Going from the hills of West Virginia to the beaches and liberalness of California was a culture shock, but I adapted.

I was a long way away from Grandma Simpson, but she kept praying that I would become revolted and find Jesus.

Penelope and I got married in 2016. The wedding was beautiful and my dress, spectacular.

I was full into the gay movement. I attended many gay pride

parades and promoted the gay agenda. "Gay Pride" is not just a statement, it is a religion and those who take part are totally committed.

Grandma Simpson, well, you know!

By the fall of 2019, I didn't want to have sex with Penelope any more. I didn't want to have sex with anybody. I wanted to want it, but I didn't want it. I had to get drunk in order to do it. I was revolted by the thought of it. I was having something like a mental breakdown. I had a 6-hour phone conversation with Grandma. I was confused and did not know what to do. When we got off the phone, she fell to her knees and prayed for me to accept Jesus. Half of her prayer had already been answered and she wanted the second half to also be answered.

Later in 2020 I called it quits and told Penelope I wanted a divorce. Within 5 days I cut all ties to California, filed for divorce and moved back home to WV.

Shortly after this, Grandma and I spoke on the phone again and this time I accepted Jesus. I confessed Him as Lord and told Him I wanted to commit myself to Him. It was real! I felt floods of joy fill my heart and was shaking! I felt His love and forgiveness…as far as the East is from the West, so far He cast my sin from me! God penetrated my cold, frigid heart.

I totally committed myself to Him. I was a new creation! I eventually stopped all the drugs for depression after I received deliverance from evil spirits. It wasn't easy and my body took some time to adjust, but now I am totally free and have absolutely no desire to be with a woman ever again.

I now spend much time in prayer and Bible study as well as fellowshipping with believers. I have a great church family who love me. God is so good and I want to help others find the truth so Jesus can set them free!

Grandma Simpson now is praying for my future husband: a godly Christian man who will love me the way God intended. So am I!

#19…One Man's Battle Against Homosexuality And The Spirit Realm

My name is Michael Eaton.

When I was first approached about recording my story, I knew immediately that everything I had gone through was to help someone else struggling with this particular temptation. In my opinion, the church as a whole has failed in addressing the needs of this particular group of individuals. Whether it was out of fear of the topic or sheer refusal to do anything other than condemn, many souls have been lost to the delusion of this lifestyle and the demonic and satanic forces that continuously attack those who struggle with this sin. It is my hope that this writing will help to enlighten you to the environmental and spiritual forces that lead one to struggle in this area. Perhaps it will also help to awaken many Christians to the reality of homosexuality and the ability to free oneself from it.

My struggles began very early in my life. From the youngest of age I can remember feeling "different." I was not interested in any of the "normal" things young boys should like. From an early age, Satan took this information and began planting in my head that I was not "normal" because I had no interest in sports, hunting, and other manly habits. I was content to read, create, listen to music, enjoy a good play, etc.

Satan used this information to his advantage by deliberately putting a wedge between my dad and me. My Dad was a "man" in the strictest sense of the word. He hunted, never cried, rarely showed his emotions, could fix anything, was in the military and was a policeman. By age 11, Satan and his demons surrounded me and constantly taunted me that my Dad did not love me because I did not fit his mold of what a man should be. They whispered in my ear that he could never love me because I was so different, that I was not the same and I could never win his approval. It was also during this time that I began to look at other boys and men and notice things about their bodies. I look back now and realize that it was natural curiosity, but, Satan began to whisper that I was gay.

I knew what gay meant but had no idea of the ramifications. One of the biggest influences on our sons is the relationship they have with their fathers. Mine at this time began to be bitter, full of hatred and incredibly tense. The loss of and/or damage to the relationship with a same sex parent is one of the key environmental factors that can affect one's self esteem and lead one into this lifestyle. If that connection is not made in a healthy, loving way, one can turn to find that affection in the relationship with the same sex. This was my case. Although at that time I did not realize it, Satan was laying significant groundwork to entice me to sin. He told me my Dad did not love me because I was different and that I was gay. I can remember first realizing how wrong the same sex attraction was and how it seemed like the right thing to do. Looking back, I should have realized that God does not create chaos and the lies I was being fed were straight from the pits of Hell. He and his demons also surrounded me with a society that was just on the cusp of bringing homosexuality into the mainstream. AIDS was in the headlines. Celebrities were beginning to come out, so to speak. All I heard from the pulpit was condemnation and that I was going to burn in Hell. I began to believe that I could talk to no one and I must be OK because society said I was. This was simply another lie from the enemy.

Satan not only uses our own thoughts but the thoughts and actions of others as well. High school was very difficult for me. I was not a jock and I was not a rabble rouser. I was a well behaved, straight "A" student who was involved in drama, school politics, and computer club. I was bombarded with demonic attacks on a daily basis and before I ever manifested it, I was called a fag and a queer. I was told that I walked, talked and behaved like a gay man. These comments were coming from other students. Although I don't know if they directly realized it, I believe Satan was acting through these individuals to reinforce in my mind that what I was hearing was true. I began to think that I must be gay because all of them thought so, society said I was and my southern culture said I was. Satan uses all of these influences on us to convince us that truth is a lie and a lie is the truth. I was not getting any counter argument from any Christian source. This was still a taboo topic in many Christian circles. So, by the time high school ended, I tried to like dating girls, but Satan had convinced me that I was really gay and there was no way around it.

College brought no relief. I was bombarded on the college campus by pro-homosexual themes, whether it was from my peers in class or from the campus administration. I once sought "Christian" counseling from a counselor at college. I was introduced, by the counselor, to the idea that one could be Christian and be gay. I was told it was ok to do both. Satan had not only infiltrated society as a whole to perpetrate this lie, but had now infiltrated the church as well. I found no relief. Satan managed to isolate me. I could tell no one. I was on my own with no place to turn. Isolation is one of his key elements in his arsenal. If he can get us to the point that we have no one to turn to, he has won a great victory. It is critical that we surround ourselves with strong Christian friends who we can openly discuss anything with and rely on them for assistance.

It took two homosexual relationships and me almost killing myself before I chose to begin to confront Satan and all of his minions who had tormented me for so long. I found a friend who was willing to aid me and my life has never been the same. I am now married to a great woman and have two beautiful children. I do not regret the path I took. I am so much more appreciative of what I have now and do not feel I would have those same feelings if it had been easy.

To sum this up, I would like to hit a few points. Though I did not encounter any obvious and direct demonic manifestations, I was bombarded with demonic activity through this whole experience. Demonic activity is not just limited to those things which can be seen and felt. Scripture says we do not wrestle against flesh and blood but against evil principalities (Ephesians 6:12). These forces do not always operate openly but more often, in my case, were very subtle so as to not be noticed. I have discovered it is the silent whispers in your ear (or conscience) that he uses against us to cause us the most pain. He takes the pain of this world and twists it to convince us that we are not who we are. He could have taunted me in any way during high school. But, he used the one area where I was vulnerable to get to me. I could have been beat to a pulp physically, but the damage done by the constant name calling and degrading comments was what he was after at that time. He wanted me to believe that I was gay by all the subliminal suggestions that were swirling about me. He wanted to use my broken relationship with my father. He wanted to use the fact that God created me to appreciate theater, art, and culture to convince me that only a gay man could do so. His goal is to take God's creation and pervert it. I was created by God to please God and Satan tried to destroy all of that with lies, subliminal suggestion, and life's circumstances.

Today, I must constantly guard my heart. I pray daily for a hedge of protection to prevent Satan and any of his demons from getting to me anymore. Spiritual warfare is a daily battle, to be fought until our dying day. It is not for the faint hearted and it is imperative that we focus solely on God Almighty as our source to confront this evil.

I always liken this to the thread and brick analogy. Try holding a brick in the air with a single thread tied to it. It will fall. Take three thousand threads, all wrapped together, and it will hold the brick. Satan does this. He does not use one single thread to hang us. He takes thousands of threads and weaves them together to create a strangle hold on our lives.

I hope that you have learned something from this condensed story of my life. I know that Satan is alive and well and seeks to steal, kill, and destroy. I also know that Jesus Christ is risen and has defeated him in every way.

#20…Molested By Many

My name is Kim Breakfield.

Back in 2019, a friend of mine went through deliverance. I wasn't sure what it was but I knew it was something that was life changing because she was so different, but I never asked about it. So, in 2021, I saw her at church and God spoke to me and said, "Ask her about deliverance." She started telling me about how her life had changed. I said, "That would be so awesome." She said, "I will talk to Bob and hook you up." I left there thinking, "What the crap have I gotten myself into?" Then I was thinking, "How can I get out of it?" Little did I know what was about to happen.

The next night at Vacation Bible School, she hooked me up with Bob. That's when my stomach did flips. Bob proceeded to ask me if I thought I had demons. I thought to myself, "If I had demons, I think I would know if I did." I said, "I don't know." Bob smiled and said, "OK."

Then I was introduced to another one of the team members. I believe that at that moment the demons that were in me started going crazy. I couldn't even look into the eyes of the girl I was talking to. She told me later that my eyes now are not the same ones that looked at her that night. She said that even my skin color was different.

So, the Friday evening that I was headed to Bob's home for deliverance, I thought of every reason I could not go and turn around to go back home. After I got there, my stomach was in knots so badly!

After I got home to do the homework paper that I needed to fill out, it was so hard to think of all the things I had gone through. To remember all the bad past made me feel like I was reliving my childhood.

So, on Saturday morning I arrived back at Bob's home and we started our first session of telling our story to the team. When I was 8 years old, I was molested by both of my grandfathers, a neighborhood bread store owner and a man from my neighborhood.

I never told my parents about what was happening to me because my grandfather had told me that if I ever told anyone, he would run the car off the road and kill us both. For an 8 year old, that's a very scary thought, so for all of my life I never knew how to tell my feelings. I had no one to talk to. I felt so alone inside of me.

So, from 8 years old until 57, I was listening to those demons inside of me telling me what my grandfather had told me that I would never amount to anything. I would never be pretty. I would be this ugly, fat girl no one would ever want. I would cut myself down all of those years.

I was sexually active from the age of 11 on into my adult life. That was the only way I felt even a little bit of love; that's how people show you love.

When I started to say the prayers on Saturday for deliverance, that's when the demons in me went crazy. I could feel their hands around my neck choking me. They would not let me say the prayer. It took forever for me to get through one of the prayers. They did not want to leave me and truthfully, I didn't know how it would be without them because they had become part of who I was.

That night when I got home and went to bed, I knew there were still some there and when I got up the next morning, I could hear them saying, "If you think yesterday was bad, just wait until today!"

On that Sunday, the team told me to fight through them and show the demons who I was and what I could do. It took a little while, but I was able to really fight for "Me" and who God intended for me to be.

After that, I became a warrior for Christ. The team and I went to our home to pray over it because our son had gotten into some bad things with Satan and called demons into our home. But, we kicked them out for good. I was able to fight for myself and my home!

I am now on the deliverance team helping others cast out demons that they don't know that they have.

I give God the glory and thank the deliverance team that is out there doing what God has called us to do.

#21…Addicted To Sex

I was a mess and had lots of problems including severe anxiety, stress, fear, worry, depression, anger, rage and seizures (pseudo-seizures) which my neurologist told me was from stress. I didn't want to work and when I did work I couldn't hold a job. I was on Prozac for depression/anxiety and I was unable to sleep. I couldn't sleep even though I was on Ambien which is a prescription drug to induce sleep. I yelled at my kids a lot and also my ex. Yes, I am a Christian but had trouble living the life. I was totally defeated.

I was addicted to sex. I knew it was wrong in God's eyes that I was having sex with many men, but *I could not stop*. I wanted to stop and would always tell myself I won't do it again. But I would anyway. Men would call me on the phone when they wanted it, even men I didn't know, and I would let them come over and use me. I didn't know how to stop.

I was always questioning God, "Why me? What did I do wrong? Am I really a Christian? I go to church faithfully so why are these things happening to me?" I could not escape my problems, but I wanted to know God and feel Him close to me.

A friend, who knew about my issues, told me about deliverance. I didn't know anything about demons or even if I believed in them. But I was willing to do anything to get closer to God and be freed from all these problems that tormented me. So, I was super excited to participate in a deliverance weekend from Friday night through Sunday night. Maybe this would help. The team of four ministered to me during that time and then another lady joined us on Sunday who also received deliverance.

There were many hours of biblical teaching and throughout the time there were a number of deliverance sessions where I repented of my sins and forgave others. Hurtful memories came to my mind that I needed to give to Jesus to be sealed away forever. Then demons were cast out of me by the team in the name of Jesus Christ. I don't remember a lot about what happened because when the demons surfaced in me, I was semi-conscious. I know they sometimes spoke through me to try to confuse the team and they frequently came out screaming.

I do remember two things, specifically, that happened. One is what a relief it was when they came out! WOW, what a relief! My mind was clearing up and all the torments were losing their grip with each session. The second one is when evil spirits of sexual lust came out of me. *At the very moment* the spirits came out, my cell phone rang and it was one of the men I was having sex with calling for another encounter! I hadn't heard from him in a few months. Satan was working to try to stop the deliverance! I did not return the call. Prior to my deliverance, I would have called him right back. I blocked him and deleted his number from my phone immediately.

On Sunday, another lady needing deliverance joined us and at one point I joined the team casting out the demons! I was amazed at how spirits reacted in her when I commanded them to come out in Jesus' name! I couldn't believe that God would allow me, a failure in life, to take authority over evil spirits in Jesus' name! My confidence as a Christian grew along with my boldness. I came to understand more fully how God forgives people totally and how He changes lives - mine especially.

It has been two months since my deliverance weekend. I sensed huge relief that first night. I was able to sleep soundly! Anxiety had lifted and I felt so attracted to Jesus. I went to God's Word and memorized Scriptures that I needed in order to keep my deliverance. I was so hungry for more of God! Evil spirits tried to come back and I cast them away in Jesus name!

Men have continued to call me for sex and I have not answered or called them back. I have blocked their phone numbers. I have no desire for that kind of relationship now. Seizures have stopped. Without even realizing it, I stopped taking all of my anxiety meds…I don't need them anymore! I got a new job and have kept it. Friends and church people I know have noticed the difference in me and have said that I look younger. They are amazed that I am not stressed even with issues in my life that are not the best yet. My pastor said, "Whoa girl! You've changed so much! You've come a long way!" I am a new person!

I want everyone to know how good God is and I have a new confidence. Imagine, the woman who was afraid of her own shadow is going door to door witnessing! That is me! I have no fear of people.

Before my deliverance, my daughter wanted nothing to do with God or church or the Bible. ***She recently got saved*** and we are doing daily Bible study! God is so good! Praise Him!!

#22…Secret Escort

You never really know what is going on "behind closed doors" with people. Such was the case with Lola. She was young, beautiful and a very successful business woman in the company she worked for. But at night, she worked for an escort service for three years. In short, she was a prostitute.

She would have sex with men, women or men and women. If the pay was right, she would do it. Eventually, she came to her senses and stopped, got married and had children, none of whom ever found out about her secret life.

Her sin caused her to be demonized and she couldn't break free of the lust and torments that came along with her sexual past. We ministered deliverance to her and cast out many spirits in the name of Jesus Christ!

This does not mean that her troubles and challenges were over. They weren't. It was now her responsibility to abide in the Word so she could be transformed. The last we knew, she was doing just that!

#23...Crack In The Soul

She called us on the phone and said, "I think you can help me." We didn't know who she was, but she had gotten a copy of my book about deliverance from someone and after reading it, called us. We don't normally invite complete strangers to come into our home, but we saw no other option so we invited her to come.

Gwen told us her story. Her father began to rape her when she was 7 years old. He continued to do so until she was 17. At this point she was able to buy a gun from the money she had earned from her first job. She showed it to him and said, "If you ever touch me again, I will kill you." He never touched her again and that event was about 40 years earlier.

After she finished telling us her story, I said, "I think you have a crack in your soul." (I had just recently read Dr. Dale Sides' book, *Mending Cracks in the Soul* (Sides,2002), but had not yet attempted to put into practice the instruction in it.) She began to sob uncontrollably! I wondered what I had said that upset her so much! Then she said, "I've known this day was coming for twelve years. That was the last time I had demons cast out of me. The minister said there was one more event that had to take place before I would be totally free." I said, "We have not done this before, but we are willing to try if you are." She said, "I know it will be painful, but I need to do it."

We invited Jesus to bring up past memories and heal the cracks in her soul. At first, nothing appeared to be happening. Then my wife, walking by the spirit, boldly commanded Satan to stop interfering and allow the Lord to do what He was going to do! Then Gwen told us what she was beginning to visually "see." She said she was seeing herself as a little girl in the backyard and was up in the tree house. She was saying, "God, where are you?" as she was pleading for help from the abuse. Then she said she was seeing Jesus by her side saying, "I'm right here. I've been here the whole time." At that point, she began to cough out demons. We didn't even cast them out, they just left! She spit into the bucket we had as she was coughing out the demons. (She later apologized for "...puking all over your living room.") The spirits that had been caught in the cracks were leaving as the cracks were healed by Jesus.

When she left, my wife and I fell to our knees and thanked God for allowing us to be a part of this!

We saw her about a year later and she was still free and living an abundant life. Praise God!

#24...Lord Of The Rings

I didn't know what to expect. I had been 'stuck in my ways' for so long that I just wanted some reprieve. When I first came up to Kentucky from Florida, I was a recent Bible college graduate seeking the will of God. Over the course of two days, the team worked through ten focal areas of ministry. Each segment took at least an hour to complete. As a result of prayer, things came to light that I had never talked to anyone about before: things I had buried deep inside. As uncomfortable as it was, I knew I had to be honest about every area in my life. In this time, I saw the Holy Spirit heal the crack in my soul. I felt demons release themselves from my body. They would manifest in ways of coughing, spitting, and numbness in parts of my body. Some manifestations wouldn't stop until the demon was called out (for example: there was a spirit of doubt that would cause me to shake).

We asked that God would show up. We prayed His will be done in my situation. We began with Scripture, and Isaiah 61:1-4 was read. I pushed back my sleeve, revealing my tattoo of Isaiah 61:1 – this is my call into ministry, to "go and heal the broken." We knew from there on out that God was going to do *something*.

The manifestations felt strongest while we were in the fear segment. Despite thoughts of where the activity might increase, this was the crescendo. I took my written notes and started speaking each area of intense fear, commanding it out and away, when my hands went completely numb. I was "used" to this as the numbness was something I had dealt with long before the ministry. My hands were the biggest culprits of my private sin – hands that cut myself; hands that surfed for porn; hands that were used for my personal pleasure in masturbation, to mention the "big three." This numbness localized itself in my ring fingers. I was silent and bent over with my head in my lap when I was quietly asked, "How are you doing, sweetie?" I tried to express that I wasn't okay. I explained what the numbness was doing, and it was quickly determined that the rings I was wearing had something to do with it.

On my left ring finger, I wore a ring that symbolized a prior commitment to celibacy turned reminder of whatever God would have for my life. On my right ring finger I wore two rings; one, my mom's wedding band to my dad, and two, a wedding band symbolizing the remarriage of my dad to my stepmom. In those three rings, one major theme echoed: sexuality. I carried the weight of generational sin.

When the rings were taken off, I instantly felt a spirit of masturbation leave me through my fingers. I had struggled with my sexuality since I was four – it was something I had 'always' known. It was something I'd held deep shame, guilt, and regret over for eighteen years; something I'd been told by well-meaning people was 'normal;' yet it was something that in that moment, whatever urge/tendency I had within me for it was gone.

I gave permission for the rings to be gotten rid of. That's when the 'thought' came to me: "Something tells me they need to be burned!" So we took the rings out back and watched the flames engulf them. It seemed wonder had filled each of us in the team – fire, with its roots in refining and purification; fire, where the Bible speaks of its use as getting right with God (such as the burning of books used in witchcraft [Acts 19:18-20]).

I sat on my knees, watching the fire before me, staring at the cross, while humming the tune to a little piece I know that simply says, *"Lord, prepare me to be a sanctuary, pure and holy, tried and true. With thanksgiving, I'll be a living sanctuary for You!"* My anxiety had melted away; I was at peace.

When we were finishing with the ministry of the Holy Spirit, I had a vision. I saw a four-year-old me reach into the hand of God, to be pulled into His arms. Ministry truths were spoken over my life, to go and do as God Himself has called. The peace inside me increased, and I felt the crack of my young soul mend.

Have faith. Trust in the power of God who raised Jesus Christ.

#25…Hot Feet

When it comes to sex, Bridget had done just about everything. She came to us to be freed from all the demons that had entered her.

She had been a stripper and she told us that in order to take all her clothes off and "dance" in front of men, she had to take drugs to get her nerve up. What she didn't realize was that when she "danced," it really wasn't her that danced; it was the evil spirits inside of her. She would sort of lose herself from the drugs and pain of lowering herself and losing all modesty.

As we began to do the prayers of deliverance, her feet began to get hot...then hotter and hotter! She said, "My feet are burning!" The demons in her feet, the ones that "danced," were not happy that they were exposed and about to leave! I said, "Back off! You'll be leaving soon enough!" The burning stopped and soon the evil spirits were cast out in Jesus' name! Praise the Lord!

#26...Chickens

When Geraldo was a teenager, he had sex with chickens.

Now you might think that he grew up in the hills of eastern Kentucky, walked around in bare feet and went to a snake handling church. Quite the contrary! He was a highly educated, former seminary professor who was the senior pastor of a mega church! He had come from the other side of the country for deliverance from his sex problems and to learn how to do deliverance so he could go back to his church and help others get set free.

Truth is he is the kind of man I want to be...someone whose shoes I don't think I am qualified to tie. He stayed faithful to the Lord in spite of the hundreds (that's right, hundreds) of Christian people he needed to forgive. He was fired from his seminary position because he confronted the leaders of it for their financial dishonesty (robbing from the till) and when I asked him to teach me something, he said, "No brother, I am here to learn from you!"

So, what's his story? When he was a boy, older men had him chop the head off of a chicken with an ax and the chicken ran around in circles, flapping its wings, until it fell over dead. This freaked him out and he hated birds, in general, ever since. He would throw stones at birds and I guess he took his anger out on chickens sexually. His problems with sex were hurting his sex life with his wife and he wanted to be clean before the Lord.

He confessed his sins, repented and forgave all those who had hurt him, especially the men who had him cut the chicken's head off and laughed at him. The demon manifestations (stomping his feet and flapping his arms like a chicken) slowly left and Geraldo was set free!

Praise the Lord!

#27…Raped By A Spirit

When Danielle told us she needed help, she was not certain we would believe her; others hadn't. The simple truth is that she was being raped on a regular basis by a demon known as an incubus spirit (An incubus spirit is a spirit that attacks you sexually.). I can only imagine what this must be like to have an unseen force have its way with you sexually.

We have run across this many times and there is a common thread; frequently, the person has a history of radical sexual promiscuity such as prostitution or stripping. A strong commitment to the Lord and determination to be free are necessary to be free.

You say you don't believe in such things? If you are involved in deliverance long enough, you will run into it and, I dare say, you will change your mind!

For Danielle, it took time and she had some backsliding on her part. But, eventually the attacks stopped after a number of deliverance sessions. Praise the Lord!

#28…Sex Spirit

A gentleman from the Sikh religion, who was living in London, reached out. I know one of the reasons Jesus came was to destroy the works of the devil, and so of course, I heartily agreed to help get this guy free. Since he was in London, which is several hours ahead of the time in the U.S., we met for the first time quite late in the night over Zoom. This man had opened himself up to a "sexual spirit" (this is how he described the spirit to me) that had provided some kind of sexual favors for him over the years. He initially enjoyed the relationship he had with this spirit, but it had become very controlling, and the man now wanted freedom. He had tried many things to no avail. I explained to him that if he wanted to be free, I could command the spirit to leave, and it must obey because I have the authority of Christ. I knew to simply command the spirit to leave in the name of Jesus and expected it to obey. So, over Zoom, I'm looking at this guy with his Sikh turban on, who is looking back at me across the screen, and I spoke (almost as though I'm speaking to him), "Demon, I command you right now to come out of him in the name of Jesus." I did not yell or raise my voice but simply spoke this command with authority. After I said this, the man said something like this, "Oh, I felt something like wind coming out of the top of my head!" I hadn't been sure quite what to expect, but it seemed that this simple command had caused the demon to leave.

He desired to be discipled and to continue studying the Bible together after this. To be honest, I dropped the ball with him as far as building him up into a mature follower of Christ. I attempted to reach out to some churches there that could come alongside him and disciple him as he was coming out of the Sikh religion. Everything was shut down for quite some time during Covid (this all happened in September of 2020 with all the lockdowns and everything) so in England no one was able to gather in groups.

I am not sure of his condition following Christ now, but I wish I had done a better job discipling him and also teaching him how to continue in freedom. We conversed over email for a few weeks. I sent him many discipleship resources and spoke on Zoom a few more times. One of the last emails I got from him was the following: "Hello brother. Tim, I am doing well. The sexual attack has stopped with the blessing of Lord Jesus. All the things which are happening because I have hidden sins or some past war experiences that have happened in my life which I was not even aware but had psychological effect on me.

If I had all of this to do over again, I would have done a more thorough process with him of inner healing and deliverance – working through unforgiveness, processing lies/ungodly beliefs, dealing with generational/soul ties etc. and commanding everything to leave prior to moving forward with other discipleship.

#29…Porn Addiction

A young man was in our Bible Study and we were talking about deliverance, evil spirits and such. He began shaking severely, and ran out of the room saying, "I don't know what's wrong with me, I have to leave; maybe it's a panic attack." He was a devout Christian with a great Christian family and taught Bible studies at our church.

The following week the man returned to our Bible study and stayed afterwards. He revealed that he had a major porn addiction, so bad that he couldn't wait until his family left home so that he could get on the porn sites. He didn't want to be addicted and controlled by this any longer. We prayed with him, he confessed his sin of sexual immorality and porn addiction, forgave individuals associated with the porn industry and those who had initially introduced him to pornography. Then we cast the spirits out and away from him. He walked away a 'free man.'

This was probably 6 years ago. Occasionally, at church, he will come up to us to let us know, "I no longer have a porn problem." Praise God!!! He is walking in God's freedom.

#30…Lust Of The Eyes

Billy had confessed his sin of watching porn and I was ministering to him along with two other men on the ministry team. As we were commanding spirits of lust out of him, he began rubbing his eyes. This surprised me and, as a relatively new deliverance practitioner, I didn't know what to make of it. So I said, "What's wrong with your eyes?" He said that they were watering because the spirits were coming out through his eyes.

Lesson learned! The demons had come in through his eyes as he lusted after porn, so they also left the same way that they came! This taught me that how evil spirits come into someone in the first place has a connection to how they leave. We must be conscious of when and how they first come in.

More importantly, Jesus set him free! Praise the Lord!

#31…I Was Not Able To Move Forward

My name is Paul Pandian from Chennai.

I was born and brought up in a traditional Hindu family. I was rejected by my family in a number of ways. They did not accept me. I was worried about my future. Due to this severe rejection, I was badly addicted to sex and struggled with mental pain. I was also addicted to smoking, drugs and liquor. I wanted to get rid of all these addictions, but something was holding me back very strongly. I was not able to move forward. Some unknown power was triggering me to do these sinful activities.

Somehow, I came to know about this Transformation Seminar and I came here. I was attentive to all the teachings and every day I got deliverance from different evil spirits. I realized that the evil spirits were the ones stimulating me and keeping me in the bondage of sin. I confessed all my sins, transgressions and iniquities. God forgave me and accepted me as His beloved son. I got deliverance from the spirit of rejection, bitterness, revenge, lust, immoral sexual desires, smoking, drugs and liquor. Now when I think of it, I am not prompted to do sex or smoking or take liquor. The evil thoughts are gone. My mind was cleansed with the blood of Jesus and it was sanctified.

Also, in this Transformation class, I was water baptized and now I am a new creation in Christ. Old things are passed away. Now I have the mind of Christ. Thank you very much for helping me to come out of the bondages of sin and its addictions. God bless you.

For more stories that include sex spirits see #'s 16, 41, 52, 57, 61, 72, 77, 87, 95, 126, 127, 133, 137, 139, 159, 160, 171.

Chapter 3
Suicide Spirits

Sooner or later we all must decide if we believe the Word of God or we do not believe it. When it comes to suicide, Ephesians 5:29 stands out like a beacon, "No one ever hated his own flesh…" If one is having suicidal ideation, then he/she is considering hating his own flesh. If, as scripture says, no one has ever done this, *then something else must be doing it*. That something else is demons. Will you choose to believe this? Do you believe that we do not wrestle against flesh and blood?

There are a number of suicides recorded in the Bible such as Abimelech (Judges 8:31ff), Ahithophel (1Samuel 15:12ff), Zimri (1 Kings 16), Saul (1 Samuel 31:4) and perhaps the most famous, Judas Iscariot. A common thread among all of these is sin. These famous people, some of whom lived at least for a while in a godly manner, turned against God and His Word leading to their unfortunate self-chosen end.

Murder and suicide frequently go together. How often do we hear of murder/suicide in the news? People who do this have murder spirits and suicide spirits. Saul tried to kill David numerous times and his life ended in suicide. 1 Chronicles 10:13 records that Saul died because of his unfaithfulness to God and because he consulted a medium for guidance. Yes, he killed himself by falling on his own sword after being wounded in battle, but the root cause was sin; he chose to rebel against God and seek information from false gods.

Suicidal ideation has become so common that it almost qualifies as an epidemic. An acquaintance of mine, who is a counselor, runs into suicidal Christians so much that he thinks (wrongly) that suicide is a way for God to allow people to escape their miserable life on earth. He will not accept the spiritual truth of the matter, that when the demons are gone, so goes the tormenting suicidal thoughts.

As I think about those who have given in to these evil spirits, including my best friend from high school, I am sad and yet angry. They could have been set free by the Lord. Instead, they chose to give in.

Let's not dwell on what could have been, but on what has been and will be as people choose to let Jesus set them free. Read on!

#32…Purple

When Cheryl arrived at our home, she could barely walk. She shook and had to be held by her husband, Jack. A friend of hers, that we had cast many demons out of, told her she needed deliverance and she knew she did as well.

As she told us her story, with great difficulty due to the spirits' disapproval, she said that suicidal thoughts had tormented her for a long time, especially recently. She would be riding with Jack and the thought to open her door and jump out was almost overwhelming. She would grab his right hand with her left hand in order to not jump out!

When Jack, her friend, my wife and I ministered to her, if we called out, "Suicide," the spirit would react and try to block her ears from hearing it by putting her fingers in her ears. As we progressed, she said she could clearly see purple on the front of her face. Not knowing what that was, we went with it and began to command "purple" out of her in the name of Jesus Christ. Within moments, she started screaming loudly and moments later we could tell that "purple" had left.

At this point she told us what happened 25 years earlier. "I remember! I was in my bedroom in high school [painted purple] and I wrote a suicide note that said I was going to cut my wrists and put my two hands in buckets for the blood to drain out." We had her confess her sin of writing the suicide note and desiring to commit suicide and we asked God to cut any connection to Satan and his demons from this. She did this with great difficulty as the suicide spirit tried to stop her and would not let her say the words, especially, "Jesus Christ." By her own will and determination, she forced the words out.

As we commanded the spirit of suicide out, it quickly manifested through screaming, even louder than "purple" did, and within moments it was gone. She said, "It's gone. Oh, thank you Jesus, it's gone." She sat back and tears came down her face as she praised the Lord and smiled and enjoyed the relief she felt. We had tears too!

As we recounted to ourselves what had happened, we determined that "purple" was a blocking spirit trying to hide the root of the suicide spirit entering which was the suicide note. When purple was gone, she could then remember, as the Holy Spirit revealed it, what had happened. With the knowledge of the note, we could then "cut" the root of entry and cast it out in Jesus' name. Praise the Lord!

#33...Molestation Leads To Suicide Attempts

My name is Evangeline.

May the Lord be glorified. Before I came to this seminar, I was bound with many sins. I had attended many meetings before but I could not get deliverance at them. Before I attended this meeting, I was not behaving with love towards others. I was suffering with anger, fear, worry, sorrow, rejection and unforgiveness. Inside I had pain, but on the outside I was smiling as if I had no problems.

When the teaching on rejection was taught, I received healing from the wound of rejection. I was rejected by my brother and mother. Because I was born a girl, even in my mother's womb itself she tried to abort me, but because of God's plan I was born. Even after birth, my mother wanted to kill me but God made me live.

When I was doing my studies from 4th grade to 10th, I was molested by my brother's friend. Though I talked about this with my mother and brother, they didn't pay attention to this matter. So, I was broken inside. Here in this class, God healed my rejection pain.

I had a heavy anger problem. Whenever I got angry, I used to beat others and break things. Even before I came to this meeting, I threw and broke my phone because of anger. This was a generational iniquity. I confessed them and I got delivered from anger spirits.

Because I was molested, I felt defiled and so I decided to commit suicide. Twice I attempted to commit suicide. I was delivered from the spirit of suicide too! I thank God that He gave me great deliverances in all the areas in which I was being tormented.

#34...I'll Kill You!

Lydia had suicide spirits along with rejection, death and murder. She was in her mid-twenties when she came to the Transformation class. During each group ministry session, they would manifest in her and as she got more and more freedom, the remaining ones got more and more bold. They tried to strangle her by having her wrap the microphone cord around her neck. They told her, "We will kill you if you try to cast us out." This scared her, but eventually she decided to take a stand and if they killed her, it would be no worse than the hell she was living (Of course, they could not kill her if we cast them out.).

I was ministering to her each time and around the 4th or 5th session, she became even more determined. The demons, in a desperate attempt to stay, screamed at me, "*I'll kill you!*" Sorry boys, I believe Luke 10:19. Moments later, in Jesus' name, they came out and she was set free!

Right after this, Lydia, through a translator, asked if she could hug me. Now that she was free of rejection spirits, she could love and be loved. Of course, I hugged her.

A year later, I saw her and the biggest smile came over her face! Oh yes, we hugged each other!

#35…Yeah! 15!

We were somewhere in India doing a Transformation class and during the first week, there was a suicidal man who was not cooperating during the class and had become a distraction. Another team member, who speaks English, and I took him outside to deal with him however we felt we should. As we talked with him, a suicide demon began to speak through him in the language of Tamil. I asked the other team member, "What is the demon saying?" He said, "It is bragging about 15 people it had killed through suicide." I said, "15?" At this point, the demon spoke English through the man, who didn't speak English, saying, "Yeah, 15!"

As we tried to minister to the man, he (the man) was not interested in cooperating, repenting of anything or forgiving people. We were at a standstill and the man left with the suicide spirit still in him who wanted to make him its 16th victim.

#36…Burned Alive

I was ministering to a man, about 25 years old, with three other ministers. At age ten, his mother committed suicide. Not only that, but she did it right in front of him. Even more horrible is that she did it by setting herself on fire! The trauma from seeing such a thing caused the suicide spirit in her to go into him. In addition, other demons, including a familiar spirit, entered.

He followed our instructions by forgiving his mom and confessing his own sins in the matter. The spirits manifested with body contortions and some verbal noises, but after, say, 15 minutes of consistent manifestations, it was apparent that the spirits had stalled and were not coming out (When progress toward expulsion comes to a standstill, something is holding them in. It could be the person is holding back something or there are more "roots" to cut.). I put a stop to the deliverance and brought him back to full consciousness. I asked him if there was something he wasn't telling us and he indicated not.

I quietly asked the Lord what was missing and a sense of compassion came over me. I felt, at least in a small way, his pain. As best as I can remember, I then said, "I'm so sorry for what happened. No ten-year-old boy should have to go through what you went through…" As I spoke, tears began to flow down his cheeks. I said, "For you to be freed from these demons, you have to let your mom go. Can you do that?" He said, "No, I miss her!" I said, "Are you willing to try with Jesus' help?" He said, "Yes." Without the person's "buy in" for deliverance, you are wasting your time.

He repeated after me and the prayer went something like this, "Lord Jesus, help me to let my mom go. I miss her, but I want to be free from these torments and live for you. Forgive me for holding on when I should have been turning to you for my comfort…" You could tell he meant what he said and then when we finished the prayer, the four of us commanded the spirits out in Jesus' name. Immediately there was a change. The demons manifested in a different way and you could tell they were ready to leave, and leave they did! Within maybe 30 seconds they left by coughing and he was set free!

#37…Suicide No More

Patty came for deliverance from a Bible college in Michigan with several demonic oppressions. I mention the Bible college because, often, Christians and even those attending a Bible college, don't believe that we can be oppressed by the enemy and have any need of deliverance from the enemy's oppressions.

A group of three ministered to Patty over a week-end. She had issues with self-mutilation, lesbianism, and suicidal thoughts. During the course of the ministry week-end very little was accomplished. While Bob was ministering, two of us were in prayer seeking direction and guidance.

During this time, I had been reminded of the Lord of my own first experience with deliverance, over 30 years ago, when a minister put his hand on my forehead and with his fingers pulled out, in the spirit, a demon of fear. I did not feel anything at the time and actually thought it was a bit weird, until I was driving home later and had a headache over the exact location that the minister removed the demon of fear. Since I never get headaches, I knew that what happened in the spirit was affecting me in a physical way. I also felt lighter and happier after that experience. It was a major awakening for me in regards to how demons can impact us physically and emotionally without us ever being aware of that possibility.

When I had mentioned to Bob that I might have something to share, he brought me in front of Patty and I did to her what the Lord had shown happened to me, she immediately started to spit up and expel demonic influences. She realized that a prized ring that was given to her by her mother, who mistreated her, had a demonic spirit associated with it. We broke off generational curses in her family line and burned the ring in a fire pit in Bob's backyard. She felt like a new person and her fears and self-destructive behavior ended.

As we were celebrating her new found freedom from these things, I had a prophetic word from the Lord that she was not going to continue in her lesbian relationship, and in fact was going to be married within a year. A year later, she was married and since has had a child.

We tend to negate the possibility of a need for deliverance. I personally know of individuals who go through deliverance periodically so that they can stay as free as possible. Noticing any unusual symptoms such as fear, or anger they ask for prayer for deliverance from any oppressive spirits.

It has been a blessing to be able to minister to people with demonic oppression and observe the changes in their lives that take place afterward. For me personally, I have noticed that I seem to get free from some minor demonic influences as I do ministry. Others have explained to me the same thing. I have also noticed that doing deliverance ministry also strengthens my relationship with the Lord, which is the most important thing for me.

#38...I Feel Like I Can Float

Zanaya was 16. She was suicidal, depressed and had long conversations in her mind with, well, she didn't know who. She had all kinds of counseling at school, church and at the local mental hospital. She had been in and out of Crisis Centers and mental hospitals numerous times due to self harm and suicidal ideation. She was pumped up with drugs that simply made her numb. She loved the Bible, but whenever she tried to go to it, she suddenly hated it. She wanted it, but then was repulsed by it.

Her dad was a doctor. He was very analytical and scientific so when they came to our Bible study at church, he was skeptical when we talked about demons. Then again, being a Christian, he believed in demons and was willing to have us minister to Zanaya; maybe this would help.

She had a lot of dark pictures and paintings in her room which were all taken down and she played video games full of killing, blood and death. She repented of all this and forgave anyone connected to them. Then, with dad's help, we cast the spirits out.

She was so different and when she got up she felt so light that she said, "I feel like I can float out of the room!" We like to hear that! We also like to see Jesus set the captives free!

Soon after this, she quit all of her psychotropic medication, on her own initiative and with dad's consent, and has not touched them in 7 years! All the torments are gone!

#39…Problems Everywhere

I was born in a Brahmin Hindu family. From a small child, I lived with my grandparents. My father was an alcoholic and a very violent man. He used to beat up my mother and my home was never peaceful. Because of this, I hated spending time with my parents.

My father died when he was only 35. It didn't affect me much, because I never had a good relationship with him. Even so, I very much desired a family of my own like everybody else. My father's mother and one of his brothers took the responsibility to raise me. This uncle went to Dubai and got saved there. He then shared the gospel with me. He told me that Jesus would not leave us as orphans. Those words touched me deeply and I decided to follow Jesus for the rest of my life in 1995.

Things began to change in my life and I got married very young. My marriage was good sometimes, but we started having serious problems. Within a year, we were blessed with a baby boy. But, as time went on, my husband and I were not getting along. We would fight all the time and it was affecting our son. In public, we looked like a very good couple, but we were both hurting on the inside. We were both becoming hard-hearted. There was no love in our marriage. Our relationship had become a responsibility. I attempted suicide three or four times and was always wishing that I could die.

I had a number of health issues like diabetes, high blood pressure, knee pain, over weight and other things. I seemed to face rejection and problems every way I turned.

My husband and I do ministry work with a very anointed spiritual leader named Pastor James. He sent one of our staff for the Inner Healing and Deliverance meeting in Salem in March, 2012. When she came back, she was a totally new person. She was a Catholic when she left and she returned a born again Christian. This really impacted me and I started to think about attending a class myself as I looked through the Transformation class manual. I prayed to the Lord that if it was His will, to let me go to a class.

I was very tired of the negative circumstances of my life. Even though I was a Christian, I was carrying a lot of baggage and burdens. I had no joy in the Lord. While I was praying, I felt that the Holy Spirit wanted me to go. I thought to myself that if it really is the Lord's will for me to go, my boss will let me off for that time. When I asked her, she said OK. So I came along with four friends from the church.

The first day sessions began and the teachings went on for about nine hours. I thought to myself that these are just the same basic teachings that we received in our own church. This continued for the next two days. During that time, not much happened. However, beginning on the third day, we began doing deliverance. I was wondering how the small team was going to be able to minister deliverance to so many people. Bro. Larry led us into confessions followed by simple prayers, but mighty deliverance began to take place.

The session on healing of wounds of rejection hit me hard. After the teaching, Bro. Larry led us into prayer and I started weeping and felt very heavy in my spirit. I made my confessions and started forgiving people and the process of deliverance began. As people began to get delivered, Bro. Larry and different team members prayed over me and I started throwing up. That went on for more than half an hour. After that I felt very light. It felt as though some heavy burden was lifted up and a cloud of darkness left me. From that day on, every day was a learning experience. During the group training sessions, I learned so much about casting out demons. During that time, I got my knee instantly healed when Bro. Charles from the team rebuked a serpent spirit in me.

The best session was the one on Brokenness when we asked the Holy Spirit to minister to us. This class was done by Pastor Joseph. This was a new level of awesome experience where we saw the Holy Spirit ministering to us and healing all my inner wounds. There was a mighty release.

I thank God for the team and for their love and care. Now I feel like a new person and nothing seems to bother me. I am able to spend more time in the presence of the Lord. Everyone around me has noticed the change in me.

#40...Many Suicide Attempts

My name is Daniel M. from Dharmapuri.

After becoming a Christian, I went through so many struggles. My village people persecuted us because we became Christians. My own relatives hated my mother and me. I had read the whole Bible four times, but I did not understand anything in it. I suffered from self rejection because I am not handsome. Many times I complained to God: "Why did you create me?" I also tried to commit suicide many times.

Because I got caught up in wrong doctrine, I was not willing to get married. Because of that, I had great opposition from my family members. My mother was also bitter towards me.

Should I attend this Inner Healing and Deliverance Seminar? First, I wondered what kind of new things would be taught there. But, when I came here I received many healings and deliverance. I learned that I was not born accidentally. Instead, I have a purpose to live on this earth. I did not know what my ministry calling was, but now I know that my primary calling is to love the Lord my God.

Many times I went to pastors to ask them to pray and tell me what God's will is for me. Now I know that seeking God and seeking to know His will is enough. I am delivered from anger, laziness, fear, slumber and generational curses. Many demons went away from me. From the second day of the class, I began to see great changes taking place in me.

One day during the class when I was praying for a person who had a demon, the demon stared at me and said, "Who are you to cast me out?" But, God helped me to cast that demon out, so I am very happy about that now.

In this seminar I learned not to worry. God delivered me from sin bondages and I am experiencing peace now. Before, I felt alone with no one to help me, but now I know that the Heavenly Father is there to help me.

During the Brokenness ministry, I received deep healing and I was not able to get up and go to the lunch break. I was enjoying the sweet presence of the Holy Spirit. This is a wonderful ministry. I pray that God should take this Inner Healing ministry all over the world. Let the name of the Lord be glorified.

#41...Tormented By Suicide

By God's grace I came to know about this meeting. After coming here, my Lord Jesus set me free from this sexual addiction as well as many other demons.

The spirit of suicide was tormenting me and I didn't know what the root of the problem was. But, during a ministry time here, God helped me find the root. My grandfather died by committing suicide. In my dreams, I would often see my grandfather coming. When we found the root and rebuked the spirit of suicide, I was freed from that demon. I thank God for the cleansing and deliverance He gave me.

For more stories that include suicide spirits see #'s 18, 19, 52, 60, 70, 77, 163, 170.

Chapter 4
False Gods

God does not tolerate the worship of other gods and the worship of false gods opens one up for demonization. When the devil was tempting Jesus in the wilderness, he offered the world to Him if He would fall down and worship him (Matthew 4:9). Jesus responded by commanding him away and quoting Deuteronomy 6:13, "…You shall worship the Lord your God, and Him only you shall serve." Ultimately, the devil wants the worship that only God deserves.

In Acts chapter 17, Paul was in Athens and found many idols were being worshiped. They had so many that they even had one to the unknown god who he told them about (the real one!). In verse 18, some of them considered Jesus, who he was preaching, to be one of Paul's "foreign gods." The word "gods" is the Greek work *daimonion* – demons. Those people knew there was a spiritual entity behind each idol. When you worship a false god, the demon behind it will enter into the worshiper. When we cast these demons out of people in India, the spirits will frequently manifest like the idols they represent…snakes, monkeys, female problems, etcetera.

It is interesting to study the word "idol" and its derivatives in the Bible. There are multiple warnings against messing with them, which include works of the flesh. 1 Corinthians 10:14 says to run from them! Stay away from false gods!

#42…Red Eyes

My name is Don Honig.
In the late 1970's, having just come out of Satanism and being a new believer, I had no idea what was in store for me as I pressed on in the deeper things of God. I was living in Puerto Rico and worked in a liquid sugar producing facility. I would work from 6:00 p.m. until 3:30 a.m., usually working alone emptying 50 pound bags of raw sugar into

a large vat to be changed from solid to liquid. I worked in a very large dark warehouse and in the center of the warehouse was a much smaller office where we had all the office equipment.

One evening around 11:45 p.m., as I was reading my Bible, the lights began to get dimmer in the entire facility. I had no idea what was coming so I turned on my portable tape recorder which had a tape of the New Testament. As I did that the tape recorder started to slow down. I didn't know why because I had just put brand new batteries in the unit. I decided to call a friend of mine on the telephone and ask for prayer, but as I started calling, the phone went dead. The entire facility had about as much light as a 30 watt bulb would give off, the recorder was dead and the phone didn't work. I turned on my flashlight to see what was going on and the flashlight went dead, also new batteries I might add. About this time I realized that I was under a demonic attack and the enemy, who I had served for so long, didn't want to let me go.

About that time I heard a noise on the roof of this smaller structure and whatever it was, it was coming down the wooden steps on the side. I could hear the beams of 2 x 4's breaking under the heavy weight. In the middle of this smaller structure was a very large glass window and as I looked out the window to the inside of the plant, I thought I saw two large red exit lights, so I placed my face up against the window to get a closer look and was taken back when a very large mouth opened right in front of me with a mouth full of needle like teeth. I realized the lights were not exit signs but the eyes of a demon looking back at me. I turned around as I heard something scraping against the wall from the outside and about 8 feet up from the floor.

About this time I realized I was in trouble: dim lights, no phone, demons on the outside and me on the inside. I thought to myself that if ever I needed Jesus, this was the perfect time, so I started to call upon the name of the Lord, not a weak, "Come Lord Jesus," but a loud cry of, "Jesus, this is a good time to show up." All of a sudden, the lights came on, the recorder started playing the New Testament, the flashlight came on and the telephone started ringing. Five minutes after that I was locking the door of the plant from the outside and quickly heading home knowing that when we call upon the name of the Lord, things happen, demons flee and the enemy is real but has no foothold in the life of a believer.

#42…I Won't Come Out!

Many times I tell people that when demons manifest, it is not like the movies...no head spinning...no pea soup out of their mouths...no real crazy stuff. But, when we encountered Ramya, well, it was pretty close to the movies!

Tom, another American, and I were ministering to her and the spirit in her identified itself as Buta which is one of the major Hindu gods. It was stubborn; it wouldn't come out. As we commanded it out, it said, "No!" or, "No, I won't come out!" or, "I won't come out of her!" Finally, it got right in my face and said, "*I won't come out of her*!!" I turned to Tom and said, almost jokingly, the obvious, "I don't think it wants to come out."

When evil spirits don't come out, there has to be a reason, so we dug deeper. We found out from the locals, that Buta and the serpent god are buddies and will sort of hold each other's hand to hold themselves in. We found out that, in fact, Ramya had worshiped this false god as well. So, she had both spirits, and later, other team members in the Transformation class were able to break their grip and cast them out in Jesus name. Jesus set her free!

#43...Come Out Of My Son!

We were ministering in India and the spirit in James was not coming out. It had given its name as Shebaraj (King Serpent), a Hindu god. So, James confessed every possible sin connected with this false god and cut ungodly soul ties. I wrestled with this thing that manifested in him openly for 45 minutes and was exhausted! Normally, I don't let it go on that long without stopping to regroup. But it seemed we were close so I persisted. James was communicating well with me, letting me know what seemed to be hitting the mark. Finally, a fellow American minister asked me if I needed him to take over and I said, "Yes!" Then he wrestled with it a few more minutes until we ran out of time and had to stop until the next day, the final day of the class, when we would resume.

I liked James a lot, so much so that I wanted him to meet my daughter who was single and about his age. He had been a Christian basically his whole life and was living it. His dad had died when he was very young and at one point James asked me, "Can I call you dad?" I heartily agreed.

I got alone with the Lord and asked Him what we were missing or what we should do. I sensed this answer, "Call him your son." Knowing that family members have more authority than others, this seemed like a good idea since I now had permission from James to call him my son even though he wasn't literally my son. Hey, why not try?

When we ministered to him the next day, the same demon manifestations occurred that had previously. Then I said clearly and with authority, "Come out of my son!" Whoa!! The spirit did not like that! The fight took on a whole new tone! This seemed to be the turning point and it was as the spirit finally came out in less than a minute and James, my new son, was set free by Jesus!

It's been a number of years since then and James is still free and in frequent contact with his American dad. Praise the Lord!

#44…Brood Of Snakes

I had never seen anything like it. It was Wednesday during the first week of the Transformation class in India and we had begun the first mass deliverance session. In the front, there was a man whose hands came together and rhythmically moved around a bit in front of him and then went straight up into the air. He put out a blood curdling scream and then collapsed into a heap.

I had seen him earlier and, to be honest, he scared me! He was big (So am I!) and had a look on his face as if to say, "If you cross me, you're dead!" Demons don't scare me at all, but this guy did.

As the deliverance session continued, he repeated the scene over and over and over. I wasn't sure if the spirit was actually leaving or just manifesting the same way over and over again. This continued during each session. There must have been dozens of times this happened.

Then during the second week, we were in small groups doing deliverance and I heard him yell out, "Praise the Lord!" Hmmmmmmm. Wonder what that's all about! That night he gave his testimony and told us that those manifestations we had seen were serpent spirits coming out that he had acquired from having worshiped the Hindu serpent god. When he yelled out, he had just gotten a vision of many snakes going down a road, running away from him. He knew the last spirit had just left and he yelled out a celebratory scream of thanksgiving to God!

When I saw him later that night, he looked straight into my eyes, shook my hand and said in English, "Thank you for praying for me!" All I saw this time was love, not fear and hate. I wanted him to be my best friend! Praise the Lord for setting this captive free!

#45…Sit Down!

I had baptized Jayaraj the day before. He was a new Indian Christian and had a history of Hindu idol worship. We were in the Transformation class and getting close to doing a group deliverance session when he slowly stood up in the middle of the men's section of the class and was breathing hard with a groan and mean look on his face! The men around him showed a look of concern on their faces because they all knew what it was: a Hindu monkey god spirit, known to be one of the mean ones, and since James was a big guy, it was quite intimidating! Monkey? More like a gorilla!

At this point, from the back of the room, came Larry. He worked his way through the men to Jayaraj. Larry was half his size with half the strength! If one looks at the flesh, he will cave in to situations like this, but if one looks to the Lord, who is bigger than all of this, he will triumph. Larry put his hand on Jayaraj's shoulder and said, "Sit down! I know you understand me; now sit down and be quiet!" He slowly sat down and was quiet! Shortly after this, the demon left during the group ministry!

Later, Jayaraj gave his testimony and said that when the monkey spirit left, he saw it walk away, turn toward him, shake its fist and then leave. Praise the Lord!

#46…Snake Spirit

My name is Raamthilagam from Chennai.

I come from a Hindu religious background. From my childhood I had worshipped the serpent god. Here I could see the serpent spirit leaving from me.

From my childhood, I was having fear problem. I was afraid of cat, dog, being alone, men and darkness. During the nighttime, because of fear, I could not have sound sleep. Now I am 31 years old. Here in this meeting I was delivered from the spirits of fear. Now I am able to sleep well during the nighttime.

I was delivered from the idol spirits. Many times I was attacked by dead peoples' spirits of my relatives through dreams. God has delivered me from those spirits.

From my childhood I was having physical weakness. This was a generational curse and iniquity. God delivered from this generational curse and diseases of stomach ache, tuberculosis, leg pain etc.

I had generational anger issue and I was delivered from that problem.

When I came to this meeting last year for the first time, I received a great joy in my heart. After I went back to home, I had a real peace with my husband and we have a wonderful married life. God blessed us with joy and peace. I thank God for the great blessings He has given me. May God be glorified.

#47…Snakes Snakes Snakes

During ministry time in the Transformation class, I was usually ministering and casting out evil spirits. However, at times, I am not "busy" so I look for other interesting happenings and shoot video. This was the case with Mary. As another team member was ministering to her, I was taking video of it and it was quite dramatic! She had a serpent spirit and it was exposed. When this happens, it makes the person act like a snake. In this case, she was acting like a cobra with both of her hands together mimicking it. She was trying to resist and the spirit was not cooperating.

Our God is all love. The Hindu gods are all hate. People turn from one god to another in search of relief and they just become more and more demonized. Mary had worshiped the serpent god years earlier and acquired the demon from it and it made her eat sand. For 22 years she ate sand! She came to the class, a Christian, still being tormented by it.

At one point, the spirit looked at each of us in the circle and spoke in the language of the person it looked at. When it came to me, it said, "Snakes snakes snakes." Since Mary didn't speak English, that was quite interesting!

Moments later it left her through coughing and she was overjoyed and gave her testimony to me, with translation, on camera. She was set free!

#48…Temple Spirits

My name is Pradeep Raja from Erode.

It is my privilege to write this testimony. I was born in a Hindu family. I accepted Jesus Christ a year ago. Then I started to search about this God. I loved God who answers our prayers. I did not have a job at the time, but after 6 months I got a job in Coimbatore. That occurred not too long before coming to attend this class. One night I had a dream about casting out demons, but I didn't understand it. Soon after that, my boss fired me, so I lost the job.

It was around that time that my pastor told me about this meeting. Because of the loss of the job, I rejected the idea. I didn't have the money to come to the class, but my pastor paid my expenses. On the first day, I felt the presence of the Holy Spirit here. During the first time of ministry, when I started breathing out, I saw a black image going away from me. I was a Christian, so I didn't expect this kind of thing to happen to me. I feel free now. Day by day, I was being freed from curses. I confessed my sins, iniquities and transgressions and I was forgiven. I feel light in body.

While I was a Hindu, I went to so many temples. I thought, "What could happen if we just go into the temple without worshipping them?" But, God opened my eyes that even by just going into the temple, by submitting to its authority, we can acquire temple demons which come with us. This was a great revelation to me. I got delivered from those idol spirits.

Many ungodly soul-ties were broken from me during this ministry. The teaching on Sin, Transgression and Iniquity was great, Larry Daddy! The marriage seminar was so clear, understandable and open hearted. It laid a good foundation for my future married life. Any true believer can become a good minister of the Lord by this ministry.

Some Insights: my character changed, Bible study method changed, holiness lifestyle came in, intimacy with the Holy Spirit grew, anger left, fear of man changed to fear of the Lord, loving people was learned, I learned to be a spiritual detective, I learned how to deal with a person who has demons and teachings on deception were understood.

Thank you.

#49…I'll Come Out In 10 Minutes

It was a Wednesday and we were about to start the first group deliverance session in the Transformation class in Chennai. I asked the Lord who I should concentrate on and He pointed out a 17 year old girl to me. Sarah was sitting near the front on the floor with her legs crossed and I positioned myself in front of her. When the leader began to command all spirits out, I said to her, "In the name of Jesus Christ, come out!" She was immediately flung back to the floor (concrete!) and began to scream. She was not hurt! I have since observed many times such things and, at times, I have a good view and can see that a violent throw of the head has a soft landing. Jesus' promise to not allow the person being ministered to to be hurt always comes true. If you are honest, you will admit that there are angels there catching them!

This pattern continued for the next week and the demon was a serpent spirit that would cause her to slither on the floor like a snake when it manifested. At one point, the spirit, apparently tired and looking for a break, said to one of us through Sarah, "I'll come out in 10 minutes." Liar!

Her mom was there too and she hated to see her daughter tormented like this and finally the Lord reminded her that when Sarah was three months old, she took her and placed her on the serpent idol in a Hindu temple in order to get healing for an infection from a bug bite. When Sarah forgave her mom for doing that, the demon could no longer stay and it was cast out in Jesus' name! Praise the Lord!

Eleven years later, Sarah and I still maintain contact!

#50…Many Idol Spirits Left

My name is S. Santhi.

When I came to this class, from the second day onwards I began to receive deliverance from weakness and tiredness. When the teaching on anger was given, I could experience the deliverance from the spirits of anger, bitterness, rage and hatred. I give thanks to Jesus for what He did for me.

During the group training, many idol demons went away from me. The family gods that my parents had worshipped were having hold in me and I was delivered from the serpent spirit. Since I am not having children, I knew something happened in my womb during the deliverance. I felt pain in my stomach and demons leaving me. Generational curses were broken off of me.

I was suffering from asthma for about 40 years, and because of that I could not go through cold temperatures. I had dust allergy and breathing trouble. I had to take the pills twice a day. But in this meeting, God has delivered me and healed my asthma and allergy and infirmities. I feel free now.

Also, still I was not able to know how the Lord Jesus speaks to us. I never received any revelation before; I could not know how to learn about this. Here I received many revelations and I received great understanding about the inner man. I received deep inner healing in my inner man.

I thank Daddy and the team for conducting this meeting. I pray that this ministry goes to many nations and brings blessing to all. Thank you.

#51...Leopard

As I was preparing to teach Bible study at church, one of the women "growled" at me. I said, "What was that?" She said, "Leopard." This spirit, which she had inherited from her ancestors who were Native Americans and worshiped the leopard, was not happy. Too bad for it as we cast it out in the name of Jesus Christ!

One of my high school students was there and got an earful, as well as an education in demonology, since there was some louder growling as it came out.

#52...False Gods Torment In Many Ways

My name is V. Murugan.

I was born and brought up in a Hindu family and I was worshiping idols in my life. One day a person introduced Jesus to me and from that time onwards I received an inner joy. Then I made Jesus my Lord and was baptized.

When I came to this seminar, the Lord gave great deliverances in so many areas. I was delivered from generational iniquities and curses which were continuing from my ancestors. Witchcraft and sorcery attacks were going on in my life for many years. Those powers were broken and I was freed from the torments of witchcraft spirits. Anger, hatred, bitterness, shame, suicidal tendency, lying and temptation of sexual sin spirits left me and I received deliverance in these areas.

I was suffering from stomach pain for about 12 years. God has delivered and healed me completely from that pain now. I was addicted to smoking and alcohol. Now that addiction problem is gone and I am free from that desire also. I thank God for the blessings He has given me in my life spiritually and physically.

For more stories with false god spirits see #'s 1, 39, 40, 56, 60, 67, 68, 70, 72, 75, 79, 83, 90, 91, 92, 95, 99, 102, 104, 107, 108, 119, 135, 136, 138, 156, 159, 171, 172.

Chapter 5
Rejection Spirits

Rejection is a fact of life which all humans will face. It can be from close relatives, teachers, spiritual leaders, friends, those of the opposite sex and so on and so on. It's hurtful and can be so painful it serves as a conduit to allow demons to come in.

Anger spirits usually go hand-in-hand with rejection. Rejection is usually a root for anger.

"That's not fair!" you say. Who are you to determine what is fair and what is not? Is anything fair in war? Well, you are in a war and it is with unseen spiritual forces and if you want to compete and not get squashed, you had better know your enemy and how to beat him (2 Corinthians 10:4, Ephesians 6:12).

Some effects from rejection spirits are unworthiness, feeling you have no value, not loving, feeling not good enough, having shame, feeling like a failure, having a poor self image, you are hindered in relationships, you don't pray, you put up walls, you reject others and sexual promiscuity.

The only remedy to be set free from the effects of rejection is Jesus Christ (Isaiah 53:3-12, Luke 4:18).

When one forgives those who have rejected him, the spirits can be cast out and then replaced with the Word of God. Take, for instance, Ephesians 1:6, "…He has made us accepted…" God has accepted us while man may reject us (1 Peter 2:1-5). He will never be separated from us (Romans 8:35-39) nor will He reject us (Psalm 22).

Frequently, the demons come out by crying: literally through the tears. Following the deliverance the person needs to be loved and encouraged.

#53…It's All Real!

My life has been completely and radically changed since my

deliverance. I am so thankful that God connected me with people who could pray with me and guide me through deliverance. After the first demon was cast out of me, I instantly knew, IT'S ALL REAL! Though I was raised in church, I still had many doubts about the Bible and a lot of confusion about doctrine. This was in part due to the fact that I was a spirit filled Christian who went to a Baptist church that didn't believe demons were real.

I accepted Jesus and was baptized around the age of 5. I always loved Jesus and desired to know him but I grew up in a divorce/remarriage home on both sides. I had a lot of hurt from my two fathers and I harbored a lot of hatred for them. My biological father told me that he never wanted to see me again and gave up his visitation rights for me, while I could never be good enough to make my step-father proud of me or earn his love. I was beat down, had no confidence, peace or true joy. I know I experienced true joy at times in my life but with all the heartache I went through, my happiness became a show and I began to exude false joy and confidence to keep up appearances. I was delivered from so many things, but a few were; hate, sorrow, anger, hurt and pain.

My life after deliverance has been incredible! Though the enemy still tries to attack me, I am not unaware of his devices and going through deliverance has taught me how to battle. I am full of real joy these days. I can see the Scriptures with new eyes and have received new giftings from the Holy Spirit and for the first time I can see the real fruit from God using me.

I was able to reconnect with my real father and his family and led my half sister to the Lord. I was able to share the gospel with my sister and she was ready to receive and so she repented, I baptized her in my home bathtub and then laid hands on her and she was filled with the Holy Spirit and began to speak in tongues. I am beginning to experience New Testament Christianity for the first time in my life. I am certain that I would not be at this place if I had not gone through deliverance to remove such strongholds in my life. Glory to God!

#54…You're Not Good Enough

My name is Christy Keith.

Most of my childhood I was made fun of for being overweight and made fun of for wearing glasses. My parents loved me but I didn't feel good enough. I remember riding the school bus and having kids scream in my ear and spit in my hair, but of course the bus driver didn't see it.

My sister was the smart one. My brother was the golden child who did no wrong. I carried a lot of hurt and rejection over the years; I was always told, "You can't do that." and when I asked why I couldn't, "You just can't."

In 2008, my world was turned upside down. I quit my job to take care of my father-in-law as he was diagnosed with lung cancer. He passed away in August and three weeks later my family life changed forever; my sister died from a pulmonary embolism and my mom was in the hospital. Four nurses and I told my mom that my sister had died. I remember my neighbor coming down after my sister passed and her words to me were "Why can't you be as good as your sister was?" I remember thinking, "What have I done wrong?"

It was hard to deal with the grief and see my parents grieving. I had to step in to caregiver mode. My mom was very ill and had a heart pump which required going to Louisville a lot and hospital stays. My dad had COPD: lots of hospital stays and doctor visits. My mom made the comment, "I could get through anything with your sister." I remember thinking, "What am I?"

I had rededicated my life to God in 2009 and got baptized. I was sprinkled when I was a baby but felt like I needed to be biblically baptized and in November 2009, I did. I was on my way to growing.

My cousin told me about deliverance. I said, "Sign me up." I carried rejection, self-doubting, self cursing, "I'm not good enough," resentment, bitterness and fear. I was a stuffer till I had enough.

I received deliverance in February of 2019. When going through my deliverance, I got rid of a lot. I forgave my parents, my brother, the ones that bullied me and those who made fun of me. What came out didn't taste good: bloody metal taste.

One that helped with deliverance came to me. She said, "You have a fear of falling." I had hurt my back and after losing the use of my leg, I had to have surgery. I fell a few times after surgery. One time I fell in the garage because of nerve damage and weakness. I couldn't get up and no one was home. My son worked a couple miles up the road so I scooted to where I could get cell service and called. He came and helped me up. But when she said you have a fear of falling, I did, and we cast that fear spirit out.

Going through my deliverance, I had freedom and I was no longer a slave to fear. The peace I received through deliverance…there is nothing like it.

After going through deliverance, we came home and cast an anger spirit out of my son. I have learned I have the power and authority in Jesus. I can cast those out: I can, and I do.

I help with the deliverance weekends too. It is rewarding to see God's people set free and see God work in us. No weekend is the same. I have learned that.

#55...Counseling Didn't Work

My issues started in August of 2019. I began to be spiritually attacked in the middle of the night. The time varied, but it would often occur in the darkest of night, before dawn. Sometimes I was asleep, and it occurred in dreams, and sometimes I was awake and it occurred in the natural realm. I had never experienced something so overtly spiritual before, and to my knowledge, no one I knew had.

I met with the elders. At this meeting, I was prayed over, but I was not delivered or anything of the sort. One woman in attendance prayed the word "love" over me and my body started shaking. I felt an inner person trying to break out. I was not freed, though, and I left there with my usual self-protective, pretend-like-nothing-happened false presentation securely in place.

All was not lost, though, as I was referred to a deliverance ministry that the church worked with at the time. I met with a woman over a few weeks, and I essentially experienced counseling. I cried for my past and the hurt that I buried; I repented of sins that I let slide; and the Holy Spirit even illuminated potential issues that I was unaware of. But in this ministry, I do not recall actual casting-out experiences.

Over the next couple of years, I continued to work through things as the Lord brought them to me. Over time, I began to feel like I had achieved actual freedom, and in some respects, I had. But I had this nagging suspicion that I might not have gotten everything out. I began to ask the Lord if He would make clear to me if I still had anything to cast out.

One night, early in the morning, I had a dream where a friend and I were standing in my nearby bathroom with both the main lights and the shower light on, and this friend (who I suspected was praying for me and this is why she was in my dream) went to switch off the main light, which caused me to panic. I did not want her to turn the light off, because I knew something was going to happen; but she flipped it off anyway, and as I lay in bed (since I had been dreaming), suddenly this dark force was drawn out of my torso and was being held out in front of me. Like some kind of symbioses, the darkness was pulled from my body but not separate, and there was a buzzing sound like an electrical hum. After this presence was visible for a moment, it eased back into my body and everything went back to how it was. When I asked the Lord to show me, I did not expect it to be so literal!

I reached out to a friend because I knew she had been working with a deliverance ministry. She sent me a spiritual inventory, I filled it out, and she and two other women helped me with the deliverance.

The deliverance meeting had the parts of emotionally processing hurt as well as forgiving, repenting, and rebuking, but it culminated in actual casting out of demons. There were more than I anticipated, and one could visibly see a struggle as they left my body. For me, they were seemingly related and included guilt (the hardest one, brought to my attention by the Holy Spirit's guidance), rejection, fear, artificiality, sadness, depression, and doubt. I walked out of the one session with spiritual freedom and lightness, a sore neck (there was struggle, after all), and an impending battle to keep them out.

The next couple of days involved standing on the truths we had illuminated and confronting pretty relentless attacks from the enemy. One particular time I was really struggling, and the Lord let me know that I needed to forgive (again), and this helped greatly. The Lord continued to show me things and bring to my mind the truths we discussed and that were clear in His Word. This was very effective in helping me (which is biblical).

Throughout this process, what I learned the most and what was most helpful to me was the idea that the thoughts occurring in my mind are often not what I thought. I thought they were my own thoughts. Much of the white noise and anxious, racing thoughts that I had experienced regularly were actually spiritual in origin. After the deliverance with my friend, it has become clearer when the enemy is literally tempting with thoughts to propel me into bondage. At times, I have not been vigilant, and they have sneaked past me as if it was just another day. But the enemy is actively trying to plant these thoughts, and they are spiritually spoken aloud in our minds. It is not some vague, overly-abstract theory. It is quite literally an attack. When Paul the apostle speaks of teachings of demons (1 Timothy 4:1, Ephesians 6:12) and Peter speaks of the enemy going about seeking whom he may devour (1 Peter 5:8), what did we suppose, that this was some metaphor? It is literal, and we no longer want to be ignorant of the enemy's schemes (2 Corinthians 2:11). This is what it means to "take every THOUGHT captive and make it obedient to Christ" (2 Corinthians 10:5). As Christians, we can pray and ask the Lord for discernment to see these attacks for what they are, and I recommend praying just that, for myself and anyone else who feels they could stand to grow in this area. Grace to you and freedom from the Lord Jesus Christ! Do not be ignorant of schemes.

#56…Rejected By Many

My name is Nithya from Coimbatore.

I was born in a Hindu family and I accepted Jesus Christ five years ago.

Before coming to this Inner Healing meeting, I had many sufferings and was bitter. I hated myself. Since my parents were not faithful as husband and wife to each other, it caused a great wound of rejection in me. I did not receive love from them. They were rejecting me. So I began to seek friends and my life became fully dependent on my friends. Slowly I became addicted to friendship. In my youth, one boy promised me that he would marry me, but he left. This broke my heart and I was very much rejected. In this kind of condition I came to this class.

When the teaching on rejection was given, I felt that each and every word was being spoken to me. When I was participating in the team ministry the second week, I shared everything to my teammates which I had never shared with anyone before. On the first day I received great deliverance. On that day I received great peace and joy from God. Though my father and mother had abandoned me, I now feel God is with me always.

Since I came from an idol worshiping background, I was tormented by a serpent spirit. When I was in 8th grade, I had a dream that a serpent was swallowing me. From that time on, I had that dream of the serpent every night for three years. I had great fear because of that. Even if I saw a picture of a snake in a paper, I became frightened. People did not understand my fear. They thought that I was just putting on an act. But that fear was real in me.

On the third day of the first week of the class, the Lord delivered me from the serpent spirit. I will thank God all of my life for the deliverance He gave. My God is so great; nothing can be compared to Him!

#57...Split Personality Disorder

Veronica had faced rejection her whole life, but nothing like what she endured from her husband. She came for deliverance.

As we ministered to her, something was different. The demons were talking a lot, or so we thought, but they were not arguing or threatening us. My wife picked up on what was going on and asked nicely, "What is your name?" "Susie." "What do you do?" "I protect her." "From whom?" "Him [her husband]." Pretty soon another personality showed up. "What is your name?" "Lola." "What do you do?" "I do whatever he wants to do sexually, but Veronica never remembers." He had forced her to do sexual things that were despicable: animals, men she didn't know, women, and so on. Two more personalities showed up with different names and all four had different tones of voices. These weren't demons; they were different personalities that developed because her soul had cracked from how her husband treated her.

After conferring with a minister who had experience with split personality disorder, we continued to minister to her. We asked the lead/main personality for permission to cast spirits out of it, assuring the personality that it would only help, not hurt, Veronica. We got permission and then proceeded to cast spirits out of each one of the individual personalities. In the end, she was much better and ready to commit herself to the Lord no matter what her husband said.

Ultimately, only Jesus can heal cracks in the soul. We lost contact with Veronica, but we know she went back to her husband. He didn't receive deliverance as far as we know.

#58...Rejection By Parents

Things weren't "flowing" like I was used to. During group deliverance sessions of the Transformation class, I was ministering to people who were manifesting spirits, but I knew I wasn't hitting the mark. Something was missing.

At the end of the third or fourth session, everyone had gone for the tea break except for one lady in the front row. I went to see if I could help (She spoke English.) and she said there was a pain in her left shoulder. I put my hand on the spot, with her permission, and commanded that spirit of infirmity out, with authority, in the name of Jesus! After about 30 seconds, I asked how she was and she said, "The same." Hmmmmm. Missed the mark again.

Then I began to ask her questions like when the pain started. She said she had it for about ten years and it started when her parents locked her in her room for three years! Since then, she had experienced rejection over and over again. She also said she waited patiently for God to bring her the right man, and He did! She said, "He tries to love me, and I want him to, but I always push him away."

With my hand gently on her shoulder, I began to speak softly near her ear. It lasted about a minute, I think, and the words just "flowed." It went something like this, "God loves you and He was with you the whole time. Jesus knows what it means to be rejected and He was right there with you too. Your walls will come down and the man God sent to you will continue to love you..." Almost immediately when I started to speak, tears flowed down her face and continued. When the words stopped coming, I asked, "How is your shoulder?" "The pain is gone!" After ten years, the spirit of infirmity was gone and rejection spirits had been cried out as well. I hit the mark! Praise God!

Shortly after this, I spoke to her with her husband and told him how proud I was of him for being the godly husband that he was (unusual in India!) and to keep loving her like he is doing because she wants it and soon all the walls will be gone. Then I prayed for them.

I had been commanding spirits out with authority, but I had not been mixing it with love! As the class progressed, I continued to take a softer approach, especially with women, and the results were better!

#59…Lead Demon

We were ministering to a lady and needed help. I was pondering what to do and had the thought to get Frank Hammond's book, *Pigs in the Parlour*, and look up a listing of lead demons. I didn't even remember if he had such a thing in his book. But when I opened it up, there it was: a listing of many lead demons! So, I began to call out demons at the top of each category. When I called out "Rejection," she went from sitting calmly on our couch, to flopping around on our floor! Then we cast it out in Jesus' name!

When "the boss" comes out, so do his underlings! Praise the Lord!

#60…Burning Head

My name is Chandramathi from Kanchipuram.

I lost my father and mother and then my sister and brother got married. I am now living alone in my house. I work at a hospital.

One day after my duty was over, I was simply resting. After I woke up, I felt that the ratio of my heartbeat was high and I felt restless. I thought perhaps that I should use the toilet and then I would be OK. However, instead my heartbeat increased and from that day on, my sleep was disturbed. Whenever I would get ready to sleep, I would remember my high heartbeat rate and then the fear of death would grip my heart.

Because of this, I went to seek help from witches and different temples. I spent about 25,000 rupees, but there was no improvement with my problem. Finally, my family took me to a doctor. After many tests, they told me that there was nothing wrong with me. The doctor's diagnosis was that I was mentally sick. I couldn't sleep for four months, so the doctor gave me sleeping medicines. However, nothing helped. My heart was gripped by many different kinds of fears. I couldn't even go to the bathroom to take a shower. I wouldn't even go to the toilet by myself. I had to have someone come with me. I was often tormented with the thought of death. I questioned, "Why should I go on living? It is better to die than to live."

At that critical point, someone asked me if I had tried different religions. They asked, "Why don't you try the God of the Christians?" So, my brother took me to a church and the pastor of the church prayed for me. I was comforted a little bit and I got baptized in water.

Even though I became a Christian, most of the time I felt a burning sensation on my head. It felt very hot, like a burning fire. So, I would pour buckets of water over my head to reduce the heat, but I still could not find relief. With much hurt, pain and mental infirmity, I came to attend this Transformation Seminar. Every day, the teachings literally made a change in my mind and I started getting hope and confidence in my heart.

I yielded to the Holy Spirit and started to forgive all the people that I needed to. During that same session, the spirit of bitterness and hatred manifested and left me.

Since I lost my father and mother and was living alone, I had felt like an orphan, feeling rejected by everyone. When the ministry team members were commanding the spirit of rejection to go, it came out through tears.

Up until this time, the demonic manifestations had been so wild. But, the day that they taught about deliverance from witchcraft, I was confessing everything related to idol worship, seeking help from witches and my own sin of rebellion against God, when a demon manifested so very violently that it took three team members to hold me. I can't describe the way the demons manifested and how violently they manifested. Finally, the spirit related to idol worship and witchcraft and the spirit of death, death curse and suicide spirit left me.

At that very moment, I saw Jesus standing in front of me with His glory. I knelt down and surrendered my life to Him. I cannot describe His glory with mere words. How great was His glory and splendor! At that very moment, the burning heat on my head was gone completely and the rate of my heartbeat became normal. There was a remarkable change in my face too. I am bubbling with joy.

This Transformation Seminar has changed my destiny. Praise to the Lord. I extend my heartfelt thanks to Daddy and the team who were serving with integrity of heart. May God bless you and use you more and more for multitudes.

#61...Growing Leg

I was struggling with sexual shame, fear of rejection, abandonment and physical pain. I've been freed of my shame and guilt. I've been returned to Jesus completely.

After a misdiagnosis of scoliosis and two years of extreme back pain, one of the team members [This is Bob...she is speaking of a team member who "coincidentally" was a chiropractor and was able to read her X-rays!] informed me I was misdiagnosed and that I actually had a short leg. God performed a miracle and extended my leg [This is Bob...I was right next to her and watched her leg grow out], relieving my pain.

#62...Deep Inner Healing

My name is S. Manjuala Jeyakumar.

Now I am 46 years old and I became a Christian in the year 2006. When I came to this meeting, since I had no money, I borrowed from others and came here. Because of over-bleeding, I was very weak and by God's grace I was able to reach this place to attend the meeting.

Though I received many deliverances here, I want to specifically mention one area. During the Ministry of the Holy Spirit into brokenness, whatever I went through in my life from my childhood: the pain and rejection by my father all came to my mind and I received a deep inner healing into brokenness of my soul. The harsh words spoken by mother brought pain to my heart and whenever I went for ministry, I felt rejected and the words spoken by her came to my mind again and again and it was a hindrance for ministry. But this meeting healed me both mentally and physically.

I want to be thankful to God for this opportunity that He brought me to this meeting and healed me. We all have received comfort by this ministry. We pray that this kind of ministry should be conducted often. Amen!

#63…Satan's Relentless Attacks

My name is Raichel.

I am 21 years old and I am coming from the state of Karnataka. I had appendix surgery in the month of October, 2017. Even after six months, I repeated the surgery because, again, I had the same pain of abdomen and pelvis which was unbearable. When the pain came, I would become bedridden for as many as 10 to 15 days. It would come 2 or 3 times a month. The doctors were not able to identify the real cause for my pains. I was suffering for about one and a half years. Finally, the pain became severe and continued for one whole month. We went to different hospitals and consulted with many doctors. I had white discharge problem and urinal infection. My blood count was low, severe gastric problem, dehydration, hip pain and spinal cord pain because of the injections they had given for surgery purposes. I came here in such a bad and painful condition.

When I attended this meeting, in the beginning I had no change of anything in my body. But during the second week, when group training was started, when I was sharing my history with the team members, after the training session was over on the first day of the second week, in the evening every pain and problem began to come to the surface. Therefore, on the second day, I even could not come for the class and training. But team members and the volunteers compelled me and made me to come and participate in the training.

I thank God that by attending the training and receiving the ministry, miraculously, all my spinal cord pain, hip pain and white discharge problem as well as the stomach pain were eliminated and I am healed and delivered from the problems. I glorify the name of Jesus Christ, the supernatural God. When I came for the meeting, I brought all my medicines and syrup which I was supposed to take: 5 to 7 pills three times a day. Now I am not taking any of the pills or the syrup. I had allergy problem also because of the medicine I was taking. God has delivered me from all the problems. The demons have gone away from me.

I had the pain of rejection and God gave me a deep inner healing to my soul. I was delivered from the spirits of anger too. Through confessing my sins and forgiving people I was delivered from witchcraft spirits. Thank you God for helping me to attend this Inner Healing and Deliverance seminar!

#64…Embarrassed In Class

We were in the second week of the Transformation class and we were ministering to Jaya in small groups. He was in his mid-twenties and a likable guy, but he had rejection spirits and we were having a hard time sinking our teeth into the cause and when we tried to cast them out, they wouldn't come out.

Larry saw what was happening, came to our group, and said to Jaya, "Do you want to be delivered or not, because you are not telling us what we need to know!" WOW! That was blunt!
He said, "You're right. I need to tell you more. I'll pray on it and I'll be ready tomorrow." This was good timing because the day's activities were about to end.

When we resumed the next day, he told us that when he was in elementary school, he had done something "bad" and was forced to stand in front of the class all day. There came a point in time when he had to go to the bathroom so he asked for permission to go and the teacher would not let him go. He finally could not hold it any longer and urinated all over himself. It went down his leg and on the floor in front of the whole class! It was terribly traumatic and he felt massive rejection from the teacher and the students. From that moment on he was rejected by other teachers, the high school principal, girls and others.

The next day, Jaya forgave all involved in this rejection, and other ones, and confessed and repented of sins he committed as a result of rejection and the demons came right out! God set him free!

One thing I learned is not to dance around issues with people. Tell them straight up what they need to do if they want to be free.

#65...Defenses Down

I thought that our family was a blessed family and I never thought of curses in the family line. Here God revealed about the generational curses and also those which I have brought into my life through my own sins. God broke the power of every curse and delivered me.

I learned about ungodly soul ties for the first time in this meeting. There are circumstances when I would repent for my sin and would forgive those involved in it, but I felt that I repeated them again and again: the same sins I committed long ago. Here I asked God to cut all ungodly soul ties between myself and the persons and through that I received complete deliverance.

I had the wound of rejection in me. The Lord helped me to find the different roots of rejection through the truth and healed those wounds of rejection and God set me free from the defense mechanisms that I had chosen and the detrimental effects of rejection also.

God helped to find the roots of anger and delivered me from this too. I was in a state that I could not forgive myself and had self-condemnation. God delivered me and made me to forgive myself.

I received great deliverance in the area of fear. Before coming to this meeting, I could not speak before a crowd because of fear. I had stage-fright, fear of men and fear of rejection. Now I am freed from these fears.

Though I had received the Holy Spirit anointing before, yet I was confused as I was taught that shouting and screaming are the mighty power of God. I would actually blame myself for not screaming. God cleared those doubts and filled me with joy. I thank God for the team that He gave me for training. In the team training I did cast out demons for the first time. Two members of our team accepted Jesus Christ as their personal Savior.

During the time of the Ministry of the Holy Spirit, I was comforted by the Holy Spirit and He filled my soul with joy and laughter. I really want to do this ministry. The pain the people had before is gone; now after the deliverance, the joy on their faces is awesome. My face is not the same as when I came here. Amen.

#66...A Deliverance Veteran

My name is Tina Oates.
I have received deliverance on more than one occasion, and

have participated in ministering deliverance on more than one occasion. It may sound scary or creepy but it is certainly not. Instead, it is very liberating! We all have been hurt or wounded by someone in one way or another. To participate in deliverance provides freedom from the bondage of the hurts and wounds that we carry. Also, there is freedom and forgiveness of things that we may have done or still do that are sins. Basically, it is open and honest communication and repentance with our Father that simply cleanses the soul and refreshes the spirit.

#67...Rejection For Being A Christian

My name is Palaniammal from Palacode.

Glory to the Almighty God! I was born and brought up in a traditional Hindu family. 11 years ago, I came to know Jesus and I accepted Him as my Savior. After that, I sometimes would face problems in my life and my family members would insult me because of changing from one religion to another. They would say, "Your new God Jesus is causing all these problems in your life." During these 11 years I was insulted by my family and rejected by them many times. With much emotional pain, I came to this seminar.

For the first 2 days I was soaked in the Word of God and from the 3rd day on I received deliverance. During the time of the first deliverance, they asked me to forgive the people who insulted me and hurt me. But, it was very difficult for me to release forgiveness. It was hurting me so much. Then they told me that if I forgive them, it is for my own benefit and the demons will not have a hold on my life any more. Then, I pleaded for the grace of God and I released forgiveness to my family members that had insulted me and hurt me so badly. The spirit of pain left me through tears. Similarly, at the time of deliverance after the teaching on rejection, I forgave the people and the spirit of rejection left me through tears.

It was a great blessing and a new experience during the time of the Ministry of the Holy Spirit. I was filled with the Holy Spirit and was energized. Thank you, Daddy, and thanks for the Transformation team.

For more stories that include rejection spirits see #'s 7, 16, 19, 31, 33, 34, 39, 40, 55, 60, 87, 90, 93, 94, 104, 139, 159, 170, 171, 194.

Chapter 6
Witchcraft And The Occult

Biblically speaking, witchcraft is any type of manipulation, intimidation or domination. In short, it is controlling people. Eve manipulated Adam; he knew better (Genesis 3:6, 1 Timothy 2:14). Ministers should never attempt to control people (1 Peter 5:3). Legalism is witchcraft (Galatians 3:1) and will bewitch people into believing lies. Have you been to a fortune teller lately? If so, you probably have some evil spirits that need to be cast out (Acts 16:16, 18). Are these statements hard to swallow? If so, study God's Word, accept it as truth and recognize your own sin and rebellion and repent! Witchcraft and the occult are dangerous to mess around with. If you are skeptical...well... take your blinders off, wake up and smell the coffee!

All occult practices (attempting to gain supernatural knowledge or do supernatural acts apart from the true God) are witchcraft. These are an abomination to God (Deuteronomy 18:9-12). They are not games to play! King Saul found that out; he died because of it (1 Chronicles 10:13). I can hardly think of a better way to get demonized than to participate in occult activity. We've done deliverance on people who got demons simply by watching others do Ouija boards and such. Stay away from such things!

Demons of witchcraft tend to be the most animated: screaming, supernatural strength and a lot of talking are commonplace when they are being cast out (Acts 8:7). The end result of casting these spirits out is great joy (Acts 8:9)! We have seen this over and over again.

The great news is that Jesus paid the price to be set free (Peter 2:24, Galatians 3:13)! One must repent and forgive those who were involved, or got them involved in witchcraft.

#68...Massive Deliverance

Arul's deliverance might be the greatest one I have ever seen, and I've seen over 1,000. He was a highly educated and successful Indian professional who was fluent in English. But, when I met him, he couldn't speak or function.

Arul was a skilled electrical engineer working for a large company and making a great living, especially by Indian standards. He was advancing in his company and had a bright future ahead. This is when things started to go wrong. Others within the company, who were jealous of his success, put witchcraft curses on him. Being a Hindu, he did not have the ability to resist the spiritual attacks. His health started to fail and eventually he couldn't walk nor even speak. He was no longer able to work and was bedridden.

His family took him to doctors and Hindu witch doctors but, as he sought help from the Hindu false gods, he only got worse.

Things became desperate when he could no longer eat. He was a vegetable: lying in bed, unable to do anything but breathe. In this state of being, one can begin to understand what it means that Satan comes to steal, kill and destroy! A gifted electrical engineer is reduced to facing death by starvation from the god of this world.

Someone told his family about my friend, Pastor Jacob, who, they said, can heal people (We know that God does the healing.) so they took him to his church on a Sunday, carried him inside and then Pastor Jacob ministered to him and cast out some demons. Arul was then able to eat, but that is all. They continued to bring him to church and, bit by bit, his health slowly returned as demons were cast out.

Months later, Arul was in the Transformation class and I met him. I didn't know anything about him at the time, but tried to talk to him. He sat in his chair and stared straight ahead. I introduced myself to him and got absolutely no response from him at all. This continued for the whole two weeks and at one point, he was taken to the bathroom (Yes, he could walk by then!) but he could not get out so they had to take the door off to get him!

After the class, and after we returned to the US, he continued to improve, as more and more spirits were cast out, and he started to talk again. Then he spoke whole sentences and his sanity returned. He even started working again as an electrical engineer! Of course, I didn't know that any of this was going on.

The next year, when I returned to India, he walked up to me, shook my hand and in perfect English thanked me for praying for him the year before! Huh?! No! This can't be the same guy! Last time I saw him he couldn't even talk or get out of the bathroom! But there he was in his right mind and talking to me!

Later on, when we had time, Arul talked to me about the whole situation and Pastor Jacob told me the story. The point Pastor Jacob made was that Arul's whole family, many of whom were in the Transformation class, became Christians as they saw the power of God that is far superior to their former gods who only hurt them. He also pointed out that had God healed Arul completely the first time he came, they would have gone home and basically said, "That problem is solved," and would have gone back to worshiping their Hindu gods. But, by healing him slowly, they all came, heard the Word of God, believed in Jesus and got saved.

This was the greatest deliverance I have seen and what the Devil used for evil, God turned to good. Praise the Lord!

#69…Seance Medium

Sherry left Friday in order to drive 4 hours to receive deliverance. Her dog died, she had to go to the hospital, her car broke down and she had a flat tire! She was supposed to get there Friday but she finally got there Sunday night! But, she didn't give up and finally made it.

She had, shall we say, a lot of "stuff." It took 45 minutes to do the prayer of forgiveness and confession/repentance. So when we started commanding spirits out, there were many!

The one I'll focus on was stubborn. At one point it stared all three of us down, one at a time, in order to try to intimidate us. Then it looked at me and said, "You don't have authority over me!" I got closer and said, "You puny demon, Jesus Christ is superior to you, He is in me, and you are under my feet!" Shortly after this, the prideful demon said, "I had Saul this way." We brought back Sherry to consciousness and we reminded her that Saul went to the witch of Endor, a medium, in order to get supernatural information from the dead prophet Samuel. Then she said, "I was a medium in a seance once." Hmmm. Ya think we might have wanted to know this?!?! She confessed her sin of doing this and forgave all involved in getting her to do it and then we commanded the spirit out. Within 30 seconds it was gone. Praise the Lord!

#70...Witchcraft Attack

It was a Monday around 1:40 AM. I received a phone call from my friend, Bala, who is in Chennai. I know him very well since 1996. At that time when he was doing his 10th grade, I was working in Chennai under a Christian organization named Prayer Garden. And there, as I was pastoring a small church during that time, he came to the church and was baptized by me. Because I had transferred from Chennai to Kalayarkoil about 8 years earlier, we had no communication. Then, by God's grace, he found my contact number and again we had the communication rebuilt.

This time when I received the phone call at 1:40 a.m., he told me that in ten minutes I am going to commit suicide by hanging on the roof fan. And he said if you don't hear my phone call after 10 minutes know that I am dead. So I came to my office room to start the prayer for him.

As I was praying in the room, within 5 minutes I received his call and when I attended the phone, an evil spirit began to talk with me through him. It said, "We have to make him like a mental person and then kill him. We are standing in the house. A magician from Kerala sent us to do this work." Then I told that spirit, "No, you can't kill him; God will protect him." The spirit talked again and said, "Bala's own aunty has approached the magician to destroy this family because of some financial disputes. Since Bala had gone to police to deal the case they became very angry against him and so they did witchcraft against him. So I will not go without taking his life." Again the spirit said. "Ask him not to read the Bible. Because for some days onwards I am trying to kill him, but because he reads the Bible daily, I am not able to touch his heart and eyes." I told back, "I will make him read the Bible more. I will not ask him to stop. You cannot take his life." The spirit said, "I came to your place now and saw you that you are praying for him. Why are you praying for him? Stop praying for him." I said, "No, I will keep praying for him; you cannot have him." This conversation with the evil spirit over the phone went on until 3:15 a.m. Then I went to bed and slept.

Then, in the morning around 6:30, I again received call from Bala and now his mother talked with me over his phone and told that around 3:30 a.m., Bala was running to the third floor of the building where they stayed and was behaving literally like mental person and wandering on the streets without clothes. She was crying saying, "Why all these things happen?" I encouraged her by telling to let us pray for him and God will surely deliver him. After that, Bala talked with me and through him the spirit said, "I am coming to see you at your place."

At 8:15 in the morning on Tuesday, he said, "I have gotten into the bus to come to your place, Kalayarkoil." It is around 400 kilometers away from Chennai. The spirit was challenging me that I am coming to see you and show my power to you and then I will take Bala to Kerala where the magician is and I will kill him there.

During the daytime while Bala was traveling by bus, very rarely he was in his own mind. For instance, one time Bala called and wept by saying, "I am wandering at Trichy bus station like a mental and I don't know what is going on in me." Then suddenly the spirit began to control him. In the afternoon the spirit talked through him again over the phone and said, "I have bound him in seven places and the only place I need to bind is his mouth and heart."

Then I began to receive a text message from his cell phone saying, "I have bound his mouth also. Exactly at 12:00 o'clock in the night I will be there at your house." Then in the evening his phone was switched off and I was not able to contact him. Then, at 8:45 in the night, I received call from him from a local phone call center and told, "Now I am at Pudukottai in a serpent's temple doing Hindu rituals." I was waiting for him with three other church members for deliverance prayer for him. But exactly at 12:00 midnight I received a call from him, from a phone communication center, and the spirit spoke through Bala saying, "I am now at Karaikudi. Because there is no bus from here to come to your place, I am held up here."

What I understood was, though he was not having wrist watch, the evil spirit was very keen on punctuality. So then I understood even the kingdom of darkness is very clear on keeping the time. I asked my friends when is first bus in the morning from Karaikudi to our area and they told 4:15 in the morning. So I asked them to take rest in the church because I know that Bala will arrive in that first bus.

While I was taking rest, I heard someone knocking at my door and I knew that it was Bala. Since he was not in his mind, I felt not to open the door directly, so I called over the phone to the friends who were sleeping in the church near my house and they came out to see Bala standing at my house door like a mental person. Then I too came to the church through the back door of my house and called Bala to come into the church because he was standing at the compound gate and was staring at us very ferociously. He said, "Just now I walked back to the main road from this street and do you know why? The dogs were barking and so I went and bound the mouth of all the dogs in these surroundings." When he said that, literally, we were not able to hear any dogs barking at all. Before that, many were barking but now it was stopped.

When I told Bala to come into the church, the spirit from Bala said, "Hi Joseph, I am not Bala. I have brought this Bala all the way from Chennai to show my power to you, and after that I will take him to the magician's place and kill him there. If you can, a thousand of you come bend my hand. No, you can't because I am very strong." I told that spirit, "I want my friend Bala to come inside the church. You cannot stop him." With a forceful push he entered the church and he was not in his mind. I tried to make him sit on a chair, but when he sat on the chair, the chair got broken. So I made him sit on the floor. When I tried to place my hand on his head he pushed very harshly. So I stopped placing my hands on him.

With the team, I sat in the middle of the church building and Bala was lying down at the door. I was commanding the spirit to leave Bala. But it was very adamant and was refusing to leave away from him. It said, "I will take his body to Kerala. The magician has given me 48 hours to finish the job of killing him. Even now he is doing witchcraft acts on behalf of him. He has sent many spirits against him. So I will not go away from him. Many other spirits like Eseki, Sudalaimaadan and Kali came with me. When they came to this town near the church location they all refused to come into this location. All of them were greatly afraid to come to this place. But see, I have even entered into this place. That means know how powerful and bold I am. I made him naked and wander like a mental. Even now I can make him naked by tearing the clothes before your eyes." I said, "Stop that action in the name of Jesus; in my location no such thing can take place." So he stopped trying to tear the clothes.

Then he said, "Do you know who I am? I am at the 5th rank in Satan's kingdom. There are four ranks above me. I am at the 5th place." So I asked, "That means you are fallen angel, isn't so?" Suddenly he got panicked and shouted, "You have found me who I am! Now you know how great my power is!" When he was speaking to me, I was binding the witchcraft spirits and commanding demons to leave. In my spirit I was breaking the power of witchcraft which was being done at Kerala.

Then, after a long time, we could see that some force was trying to drag Bala's body outside of the church building. Since I was not near him to stop him from going away from the building, I was commanding the angels to come and do the battle with the fallen angel. For a long time as he was lying down. We could see his body was being pulled here and there. He was shouting, "Leave me, and leave me alone!" I know the holy angel was pulling Bala's legs inside the building and some other forces were trying to pull him to take his body outside of the church by pulling the head. It went on for some time and during those hours I was commanding and binding the kingdom of darkness and my team was praying in tongues.

Then finally, at 10:40 a.m., I knew in my spirit that the battle had been won. Suddenly he fell on the floor unconscious. Then I went near and called Bala to bring him back to his consciousness. When he woke up he saw his own dresses and his body and cried not understanding what had happened. He asked for food because he hadn't eaten for 6 meals. So we provided coffee and breakfast. After he had a shower and we bought a new dress for him, he was happy and went home to Chennai in the night. All glory be to God the almighty alone!

After three days, again that magician resent the witchcraft attack towards him. This time also, Bala called me over the phone and the spirit inside him spoke with me through him challenging me, "First time you stopped me and defeated me. I have already sacrificed 14 humans. Now again I have sacrificed 3 more young persons and used their blood to have more power to fulfill my task." At that time the spirit was threatening me and told that it would kill me if I continue to interfere in its work. I told, "This is my God-given ministry, so I will not stop. I will keep on doing it. I am not going to be afraid of you." Then the third time the spirit of the magician spoke through Bala and began to say, "Now my aim is not on Bala, but on you only; come let us do the battle." But I said, "It is not me but my Jesus will fight for us. I am standing behind and He will defeat you." Then he began to offer me saying, "You stop praying for this Bala. If you do, I will give 10 acres of land in Chennai; I will make your name famous in main cities and in western countries by publishing about your name as a famous person of deliverance." I could sense the spirit was trying to deceive me by offering popularity and prosperity. So I said, "I am not going to fall into your temptation. My desire is my Jesus should be glorified and His blessings are enough for me." Finally he was defeated and Bala is doing well now.

My personal words: because Bala had unforgiveness against his aunt's family for cheating his father and took his father's money, the kingdom of Satan had entry point into him. In this situation, witchcraft power also joined together and had more effect of attack. Fallen angel was assisting the witchcraft act to be more effective for satanic kingdom works to be carried out. Unforgiveness and vengeance had the entry points in him for the kingdom of darkness to have its attack on him.

#71...Seeking Help From A Psychic

We got an urgent phone call from a Christian young lady who was terrorized because her home was full of spirits. She had gone to our church out of desperation and they provided her our phone number.

We met with this young lady and learned that her grandfather had recently passed away and she missed him so much she wanted to talk to him. In her 'need' she went to a psychic to see if she could help.

After going to the psychic, her home became majorly demonized, things on their mantle would move, furniture be repositioned, and she was SCARED! When we talked with her she asked, "Was that wrong? Did I do something I shouldn't have?" We discussed the powers of the darkness, and why that was not a good idea. She told us things got so bad, she had gone back to the psychic a second time, who sold her 2 candles for $200 to get the spirits out...that didn't work and it got worse...the psychic told her they would have to come do a total exorcism on her home and that would cost $2000.00. She and her husband did not have that kind of money, so she came to the church. We told her that we didn't charge anything, but in the name of Jesus we would cast those spirits out...and guess what? Those spirits left in the name of Jesus!

#72...Satanic Sex Abuse

In June, 1991, in Edmonton, Alberta, we had an outreach choral presentation hosted at our church building. A lady drove up and parked in our lot quite by accident (humanly speaking) and one of our good elders convinced her to come in and hear the concert. Mimi was 40ish... going on 70, a short, stout woman who had no discernible strength. There were about 15 steps up from the parking lot level to the sanctuary level. She slowly ascended the steps stopping every 3 steps to catch her breath. Her appearance was odd. She sat there hanging her head down, never looking us in the face. She occasionally turned her head to the side and glanced at us. We didn't know what to make of that. Some of my good deacons spoke to her kindly and we found out that she lived 50 miles away and was in town for some doctor's appointment both that day and the next. She had diabetes and heart issues that the doctors were watching.

She did stay for the concert and at its end she asked if she could come in and speak with me, the pastor, in the morning, so we set up a 9 AM appointment. The Friday morning appointment was an amazing experience. In her slow, careful way she struggled to tell her life story. Mimi had been raised in a Satanic house where from age 18 months old and on she was used for sexual favors of men. At age 3 she hurt so badly, both physically and psychologically, that she cried out to "god" for help. Spirit beings appeared in her room with her to console her and acted with pity toward her. They asked her if she, "…would like someone to come inside of her and live in her to help her?" She happily agreed.

From that point on, Mimi was possessed [demonized] by many demons or "guardians" as they called themselves. I didn't know what to do with her and her story...so I did what any pastor would do, I said, "Let's pray." I reached across the desk and held her hands and prayed for her and her tough situation. As I prayed for her some of the demons in her vocally and visually surfaced and tried to stop the conversation. I say, *visually*, because I could see in her eyes that there was something else inside of her using her eyes to look at me. This is very hard to describe. For a while I spoke to the demons—even argued with them. They corrected me and said they were "guardians" not demons. I told them to leave her alone, but I was at a loss as what to do. I had always believed in the existence of demons, I just had no training in what to do if I was confronted with them.

Thankfully, my secretary heard the conversation through the open office door and called a number of church members asking for their immediate prayer for the spiritual warfare going on in the office. Then she brought our custodian, Harold, into the room. Harold is a big guy and he had some experience with demon confrontation in other churches. As he came into the room he said, "In the name of Jesus Christ, demons, shut up!" And to my amazement...they shut up! Then we tried to talk to Mimi and asked her about faith in Christ. The demons occasionally interrupted and we shut them up in Jesus' name. I'd ask her, "Say, 'I love Jesus.'" She'd try to, but the demons would not let her say the name of *Jesus*. When she tried she would crumble in pain—her arms and head hitting the desk top. Later she told us that when she tried to say the name of Jesus that they would squeeze her heart causing severe pain—she thought she was having a heart attack.

During this time, 3 times the demons tried to get Mimi out of the room. They caused her to stand up (by this time our youth minister had joined us) but the 3 of us forcefully pushed her back into the chair. By the way, it took **all** of our *strength* and *mass* to force her to sit down, three times! Finally, Harold commanded the demons to leave her in the name of Jesus Christ, and they did; it seemed.

That afternoon we immersed her into Christ upon the confession of her faith in Jesus. It was such a delight to talk to her... she was so different. She was able to articulate how much she loved Jesus, how she had always wanted to become a Christian, but no one helped her do so. When she was in town she would go and sit in various sanctuaries, hoping for help. But she was always asked to leave because of her strange body language...I suspect ministers may have thought she was drunk or on drugs.

She came to church on Sunday and we introduced her to all as a new sister in Christ. She came back by on Monday morning to say goodbye. Goodbye? It seems that she was leaving in a few days on a 4-month trip down through the southern US with a lady friend. We had a great time of encouragement, then I had prayer for her as she was about to leave. That was when she had more demons surface in her and vocalize their anger at me and what was happening to her. Man was I surprised. But having learned the lessons of Friday, I prayed for her and commanded the demons to leave her in the name of Jesus—and they did. It is hard to explain, but she and I talked for a while after this and she was even *better*, more delighted in the Lord and on fire. I think the explanation of why there were still demons in her that hadn't been cast out was that we did not command **all** *the demons in Maria to leave in the name of Jesus.* Since only some of the demons had engaged us in discussion on Friday, only those were required to leave. These other demons must have "hid out," that is, not surfaced. So I have learned the lesson to make sure in exorcism that you command "every" and "all" demons in a person to leave in the name of Jesus Christ."

#73...15 Chair Demon

There are times when something happens that catches you off guard. This was one of those times.

We were about to start the group deliverance session on

witchcraft. I was sitting in the front and happened to be looking to the right, where all the men were sitting, when the command came for all the demons to leave in the name of Jesus Christ. I was looking right at him and he jumped from his seat, flew through the air, and landed in the row behind him, all the while thrashing and spinning! I hesitated, from surprise, and watched as plastic chairs went flying in all directions! Within moments, several team members were on him and took control, commanding the spirits out and they came out. This came to be known as the "15 Chair Demon" since about 15 plastic chairs had, shall we say, lost their place!

The man was set free and testified about it later, apologizing for the commotion that he caused while we assured him we knew it wasn't him! Praise the Lord!

$74…Cards Anyone?

November, 2016 –

I had gone to a work conference in Louisiana. While there, the entertainment one night was the Mardi Gras World with dinner afterwards. At dinner, the entertainment was tarot readings and I was the first one there in line. From that time until entering Bob's class in January 2017, I was troubled, depressed, found little pleasure in work and was having problems completing daily tasks that before I took pleasure in and was thankful to do. My devotions were not on track and something was off –

January was the Daniel Fast and I was looking forward to that and finding answers for "getting back on track with what the Lord had in store and daily routines." In my head I was thinking "menopause is horrible." Could that be it? My husband, Allen, and I were looking for a Sunday school class for the spring session. Bob Hammond was teaching about how Scriptures come alive, studying God's Word, and its application to our daily walk. That sounded like what I needed.

The first class we attended, we learned very quickly about Bob's work in deliverance and casting out demons. What?! In this day and age? Not thought about that. There were 2 other ladies in the class that shared their personal experiences of deliverance. I was searching for ways to be closer to Christ and all of a sudden I did not want anything to separate me which is exactly what I had been feeling and experiencing: separation. Something was causing me to be divided and that would not work.

I shared about the tarot cards, and I knew that was wrong. I asked for forgiveness and prayer. I remember feeling so tired and uncertain of any change at first. On the way home I kept praying and felt pain in my temple and then my head. I did not stop until I entered the house and grabbed Allen and told him what was happening and he continued to pray and call on the name of Jesus placing his hands on my head. I was coughing and crying at the same time. I remembered Bob said that in the name of Jesus, cast out anything that was there, and whatever had come out to leave the house and never return: my physical being, my family and the house, go away IN THE NAME OF JESUS.

Wow! Thank you Lord, for forgiveness and renewal. I was evidencing God's mercies back at work and at home. I have changed, grown, made mistakes, learned from mistakes, had the privilege of being on Bob's deliverance teams multiple times and thankful to share that God is great and rich in mercy and love.

#75…Witchcraft Curses

My pastor got angry and cursed me saying, "Wherever you go, your ministry will not flourish. You are not going to build a church or ministry. Souls will not be added to your church." After I started doing the ministry in various places, I could not see any fruit from my ministry. I was just like my pastor's pronouncement.

In 1991, I was baptized with the Holy Spirit and in 1996, I got married to a partially blind girl. God gave us two beautiful children.

My mother suffered a lot under the powers of witchcraft and became mentally sick. She developed ulcers and died in 1998. To restore the health of my mother, my father did blood sacrifices, used witchcraft objects and did many rituals. But, those things didn't save my mother. Thus we were under the generational curses. So, with much depression and oppression, I came to this meeting.

The teachings in this class pinpointed to me that I was going away from the will of God. I discovered that it was important for me to repent of many things in order to receive my healing. I had wandered away from my first love. I started to confess my sins and decided to forgive the people who had hurt me badly. I especially forgave my pastor, who had cursed me and I broke the power of his evil words. At that time, the spirit of unforgiveness left me through vomiting.

I pleaded for the mercy of God. I confessed the sins of my father for doing blood sacrifices and rituals. I also asked God to forgive me for worshipping idols. God forgave me and the evil spirits came out of my body through coughing and yawning. I was totally delivered from many years of depression and oppression.

Now I feel lightness in my body. I am happy. The group sessions were very useful for me. I was able to open up many things in my life that had been hidden for a long time. It was like a cleansing of my soul. Praise the Lord. May God bless you and your team.

#76...The Hulk

Arun was a pretty big guy. So, other big guys ministered to him to cast out evil spirits. As the demon began to manifest, it started dragging one of them around with him then 1...2...3...4...5 guys! He dragged 5 guys around the room with him while he was screaming! It reminded me of the movie *Jaws*; it didn't seem to matter how many barrels were hooked into him, Jaws could take them under water. That was Arun! He had super human strength, but like all evil spirits, it couldn't hurt the men ministering to him and eventually it left and Arun fell into a heap, delivered once and for all in Jesus' name from that spirit.

Later, he testified that he had previously been deep into witchcraft and it was a witchcraft spirit that had been cast out. Witchcraft spirits are known to be more animated than most.

#77...Witchcraft From Jealousy

My name is Charles.

From a child, I was addicted to immoral sexual lust and alcohol. I struggled with them, but could not overcome them. During this class, I confessed my lustful thoughts and repented for my evil doings and the demons came out through my eyes. All the rest of the days I was here, I had no more immoral thoughts and no more driving pressure to go get what I had been addicted to.

Some of my relatives were jealous of me and my family. They wanted to either murder me or for me to commit suicide. So they went to a witch and paid him only 3 Indian rupees [about 4 cents] to do witchcraft against me. Because of this attack from witchcraft, I tried to commit suicide many times, my family became divided and we had no peace in our family. Almost every member of my family was tempted to commit suicide. We were severely attacked by the spirit of death.

In the class, during the teaching about witchcraft, the Holy Spirit reminded me of the things that had happened to me and my family through that witch. I forgave the witch and the people who paid him to do the witchcraft. At that time, the spirit of witchcraft manifested very powerfully. No one was able to control me. The team members finally helped me to get delivered from that spirit that was sent through witchcraft.

I was also attacked by a death curse that was pronounced on me by my church pastor. My pastor had said to me, "God did not accept Cain's offering and it is the same with you." From then on, I suffered a financial crisis. I didn't know that it was a curse. I worked hard, but there was no blessing in it for me. I kept having to spend my money in ways that I didn't want to. I could not discover why I was having this problem. But, during the class on Blessings and Curses, the Holy Spirit reminded me to forgive my pastor. I forgave him and both the spirit of death curse and the spirit of financial curse came out of me. Praise the Lord.

The teaching on Giving laid a foundation for me to begin to receive my financial blessings. Thank God for the healing and deliverances that He has given to me and my family.

God bless Daddy and his team.

#78…Little Shop Of Horrors

We have had two shops here in town since we have lived here that advertised psychic readings and other such divinations. The first may have been in business before you [Bob] left or just shortly thereafter.

One night we were discussing superstitions. Specifically, we said a Christian should not read or discuss horoscopes, visit psychics, or practice any other superstitious activities and it reflects a rejection of God's providence in and over our lives in that we are consulting other mediums for direction or influence in our lives. In our Bible study we talked about King Saul and his consulting the witch to talk to Samuel as an example that there are consequences for disobeying God and not seeking Him first. We also referenced Leviticus and Deuteronomy about not consorting with those who practice divination. One of the attendees wanted to know if it was wrong if the purpose was intended for good like the police seeking a psychic to help find someone who is kidnapped. The answer was obviously no.

That led us to agree to pray against the spirit of divination of the person that was operating the psychic shop so that no one else would be led astray and that she might come to receive the Holy Spirit and be saved. Every night on my way home I would speak against the spirit of divination and pray that it would be cast out. I always felt bold and that I spoke with authority in Christ's name. All of us in the group continued to do that until it closed later that summer.

A second shop opened a year or so later. We took up doing the same thing. I passed that one much less frequently than the first store but am pleased to report it also has closed. Praise be to God!

#79…Wild Manifestations

My name is Hepzibah Ruban.

I came to this deliverance ministry from Chennai. I was born and brought up in a Hindu background. Then I received the gift of salvation and became a Christian. The torment of evil spirits was going on in my whole family. From the year 2010, the torments became wild and manifested openly. My father and my mother's background are witchcraft and ancestral worship. I also had worshipped idols. We were going through severe curses. We went to many places for freedom but we could not find it. In March, 2018, I learned about the need of confessing sins for deliverance and I began to receive it little by little. Before, I had attended a mini-seminar of this class for 3 days. At that I tasted the deliverance.

In the 12-day seminar that the Lord brought me to, I came with a broken condition and tears. Every day I received great deliverance through truth that was taught. I threw up blood during the ministry time and demons left me.

On the last day during the Ministry of the Holy Spirit into Brokenness, I received greater deliverance. I could see demons leaving me and going away. These were not dealt with before in the previous 11 days. The demon which had taken root when I was in my mother's womb left me and I was delivered. In my spirit I was taken up into heaven and I could see the throne and the One sitting on the throne. I saw myself standing in a white robe worshiping with the angels. During that time the Holy Spirit was giving inner healing and comfort to me. This is the first time I had this experience and it was of great joy. I give many thanks to God our Lord. I thank God for this ministry.

#80…Hissing Snake

I am involved in the Healing Rooms ministry. It was 9 pm and we were just about ready to leave when the receptionist came back and told us there was a girl who wandered into the building who seemed confused and said she saw the sign while driving by that said "Healing Ministry" and felt like she was supposed to stop at this church!

We took her back in a room and she gave us a little background of what was going on. She said she was involved in a relationship with someone that was involved in witchcraft and she was hearing voices in her home and objects were moving in the room. She seemed incoherent and I thought maybe she had a mental illness as she was very scattered in her thinking! She explained that she had to leave the home she was in and just started driving and did not know where she would go but thought if a church was open she could go in there as it represented safety to her. She ended up 20 miles away and when she saw the sign outside the church, she stopped as she felt an inner voice was telling her to go in and ask for help!

When we began to pray for her, she turned to me as I was sitting on her right and locked eyes with me in one of the most chilling looks of hatred I have ever encountered! I felt a chill go down my spine but told myself not to fear because we have God-given authority in the name of Jesus!

The team started calling witchcraft out and she bolted for the door but one of the team members stood in front of it and would not let her out! One by one demons were called out and the process was lengthy and with shouts and screams. She started slithering around the floor like a snake with hissing, etc. When I looked down at her, she had a tattoo at the small of her back that said, "Sweet Seduction." When that was called out as a seductive spirit she collapsed on the floor! After she laid there for awhile this girl who was totally incoherent got up like the demoniac that Jesus cast out spirits from and was in her right mind!

She sat down with us and began to sing songs of praise that her grandmother taught her in a beautiful voice. We all praised God together with her and left in amazement in what God had done!

#81...Not Herself

Over the years I've been invited to preach in many churches and frequently am asked to return. Such was the case in 2006. By then, I knew many of the people there and was in contact with some of them by email.

I had gotten to know Christina and her family, and she had been very helpful and loving with the children in the church when we came to town to do ministry. However, when I returned, a year later, she was different. She had dark clothes on, wore dark sunglasses, had become distant, didn't talk to anyone and didn't smile anymore. I was told that for maybe six months she had been dabbling in witchcraft having become disillusioned after failing to be accepted into the college she wanted to attend. She was 18 years old and had lost her purpose for life. She went to church only because her parents made her go and because, on that Sunday, I was there.

After church a bunch of us prayed together in a circle. Christina was in it. I then asked her parents if I could pray with her alone. They agreed. I took her aside privately and told her how much I appreciated what she had done for the children in the church and how she was the kind of young lady I wanted my son to meet and so on. I could tell she wanted me to pray for her and that she wasn't just letting me in order to please her parents. Then I prayed for her. Before you knew it, she was crying. She missed who she really was and was embarrassed for what she had become and wanted to be free again. I cast the spirits of witchcraft out of her in the name of Jesus Christ.

Five minutes later I was on my way home and shortly after my return I got an email from the pastor, "She's back to her old self!" About a year later I returned and her mom caught my eye and with a smile motioned with her head toward Christina. I mouthed, "I know!" There she was, just as vivacious as ever with the joy of the Lord all over her!

She eventually did graduate from college and married a great Christian man who is a highly skilled professional. They have two kids and are thriving. Jesus came that we might have a more abundant life and Christina is living it! Praise the Lord!

#82…Delivered From Witchcraft

My name is Pathmavathy from Chennai.

I faced lots of obstacles even when trying to come here. But, by overcoming them I was able to get here. Even my children told me not to come, but God helped me by removing the obstacles.

I was suffering with witchcraft problems. My children didn't have peace of mind because we were having so many family problems. I had attended many fasting prayers in Chennai for receiving healing and deliverance. But I did not receive. One of my friends asked me to come for this meeting. On the first day I did not like the meeting. I was asking those who were with me to find a bus so that I could go home. But when the second day of class began, I started to like the class. It became very interesting. According to the verse, "…you shall know the truth and truth will set you free," I experienced that verse to take place in my life. I received deliverance and healing, and I saw all the people receiving miracles and deliverances.

I will tell others what I have experienced. On these six days I forgot the problems with my children and home. It was great and glorious. I give many thanks to the Lord. I will pray for the team. I was delivered from the spirits of fear and witchcraft. I was delivered from a human spirit also.

For more stories with witchcraft and occult spirits, see #'s 28, 52, 60, 63, 84, 93, 131, 140, 144, 154, 156, 159, 170.

Chapter 7
Generational Iniquity

Iniquity is repetition of sin: a habit pattern of having a perverse way of thinking or behaving. Thirteen Scriptures in the Old Testament say generational iniquity is passed on to family members from ancestors to generation after generation (Exodus 34:7). It can be virtually any kind of sin from anger to sexual immorality to poverty.

A person must confess the iniquities of the ancestors and repent of them in order to be free (Nehemiah 9:2). We have seen this freedom come time after time. We also see family members, offspring of the person we are ministering to, receive deliverance and wonder how it happened! We've even seen it go up the family line!

Physical infirmities can be caused by generational iniquities that medicine does not have an effect on (Jeremiah 30:12-14). Many times we seen people spend all their money to fix a physical problem but it never gets fixed until the person repents of the iniquities of his/her ancestors. A notable physician, who has practiced medicine for over 50 years, told me he has encountered many patients who never seem to be able to break free of a physical condition. He has referred people to us for deliverance!

Don't hesitate; confess your iniquities and those of your ancestors and let Jesus set you free!

#83…Cannibal

Just when I least expect it, I will run across a situation I haven't seen before. This was one of those times.

We were doing deliverance with Ron who had a very strong Native American background as all four of his grandparents were full blooded Native Americans from various tribes. He was proud of some of the family traditions and repentant for others such as the worship of false gods (animals). Many spirits were cast out of him.

At the end of one of the sessions, I was walking out of the room when Ron said, "I don't think I told you that my family once practiced cannibalism."(When a warrior would kill his opponent in battle, he would cut his heart out and eat it.) I immediately turned around, pointed my finger at him, and said, "Let's deal with that right now!" He started shaking hard! As he shook, we had him forgive his ancestors for doing this and then we cast out the cannibalism spirits of generational iniquity. He said, "WOW! That was powerful!" Yes, and Jesus is more powerful! Glory to God!

#84…Screamer

The room was relatively quiet as we were getting ready for a group deliverance session when suddenly a lady in a seat by the aisle fell to the floor and began to scream with a familiar "demon" type scream. I was close to her and went to her side and said, "Be quiet! You'll be coming out soon enough!"

When we finally got to the deliverance, a spirit of generational witchcraft from her grandmother came out of her.

Later on, she told me that she knew there was some sort of generational curse on her and then she remembered that her grandmother had practiced witchcraft. As she was writing this down, the demon in her saw what she was writing and then screamed because it knew the gig was up! It couldn't "read her mind," but it could see what she wrote!

#85…Generational Spirits In Action

Francis, the pastor who runs an orphanage, was teaching me all week what deliverance looks like in his country. I knew there were strong demonic powers taking place in Sierra Leone as I've heard plenty of stories of these powers at work. But this time, Francis showed me video after video he has taken as he is casting out demons. He takes these videos to show the person who is being attacked what happened during the deliverance as they are unaware. I saw, with my own eyes, demons speaking to him, shrieking at the name of Jesus, just like Luke describes in Acts. Francis asks the demons how they got into this person, and many times it is because of a generational curse – the parents or grandparents dedicated their kids or grandchildren to Satan, sometimes to gain basic necessities like food or water. The demons tell him things no one would know. Many times this information happened before the person was even born.

Spiritual warfare is a real thing. We experienced it and now I know what it looks like. The good thing is now I know how to combat it. Putting on the armour of God, as described in Ephesians 6:10-18, is necessary to combat evil. Look at the world around us…evil is abounding in all kinds of forms. See it for what it is.

The day before we left, my husband went to the school and talked to two classrooms of senior students, encouraging them and sharing the Gospel. He then had a meeting with our football (soccer) team (Joy Football Club) encouraging them and also sharing the Gospel. He then met with the coach of the football team, and personally shared the Gospel with him. After this, he came back to the house and said he wasn't feeling well. He lay down and got a really high fever. We have no way to know how high the fever was, but it was concerning. He stayed in bed for several hours, got up, felt better, then danced with the kids. That night the fever returned, along with my anxiety, in an extreme way. All I could think about was my husband dying in a foreign country. My prayer warriors laid hands on me, praying away all the sickness I was feeling along with my anxiety, and Jim's prayer warriors were laying hands on him. We were a mess! But sharing the Gospel 4 times in a matter of hours and extreme sickness lead us all to believe there was some spiritual warfare going on.

I have a very long way to go in my spiritual journey. I feel like scales have been removed from my eyes. I am so grateful for a team of people I got to spend 10 days with who are way more spiritually mature than I am, and I can learn from them. It is a gift to hang out with people who make you a better person and a stronger Christian. Surround yourself with those people, then become that person, then surround yourself with people who need it. What if the church looked like it did in Acts…can you even imagine what we could do?! BE THE CHURCH IN ACTS! Don't wait for others to be that church. YOU be that church! Pray fervently, out loud, and use the powerful name of Jesus. Cast out and rebuke anything that is not of Jesus. Repent. And watch the peace that passes understanding take over your life. It's life changing.

A final word: Be strong in the Lord and in his mighty power. Put on all of God's armor so that you will be able to stand firm against all strategies of the devil. For we are not fighting against flesh-and-blood enemies, but against evil rulers and authorities of the unseen world, against mighty powers in this dark world, and against evil spirits in the heavenly places. Therefore, put on every piece of God's armor so you will be able to resist the enemy in the time of evil. Then after the battle you will still be standing firm. Stand your ground, putting on the belt of truth and the body armor of God's righteousness. For shoes, put on the peace that comes from the Good News so that you will be fully prepared. In addition to all of these, hold up the shield of faith to stop the fiery arrows of the devil. Put on salvation as your helmet, and take the sword of the sprit, which is the word of God. Pray in the Spirit at all times and on every occasion. Stay alert and be persistent in your prayers for all believers everywhere. (Ephesians 6:10-18 NKJV)

#86...Ax Murderer

I have heard it said that there is no proof of generational curses being passed down through family lines. Can I go ahead and provide proof that they do? I was there; I saw it.

Latha was about 30 years old. She had always had extreme pain in her right hand. She spent all her money on doctors, but they could not help. No medicine helped or any other treatment. Her right hand simply hurt...all the time.

When she heard about generational iniquity and curses, she remembered that years earlier, before she or her mother were born, her grandfather had chopped the right hand off of her grandmother with an ax! So, she forgave her grandfather for doing this and cut any ungodly soul ties between her and her grandfather. When she did this, her hand stopped hurting for the first time in her life. She was healed! I was there; I saw it. Praise God!

May it never be said again that there is no proof of generational curses being passed through family lines. There is.

#87...Generational Anger

My name is Leema Rosy.

I thank God for this meeting. My family and I have a Roman Catholic background. Now my Mom and I are baptized and we believe in Jesus Christ. Though I am a Christian, I was not focusing on reading the Bible and I was not praying enough. When I came to this meeting, I was not ready to come here. I had double mindedness of whether to go or not. My Mom and I came here for this meeting. I had no idea about deliverance or what it would be like.

This is the first time that I attended the deliverance meeting. Actually, I came here for Mom's sake only. But God delivered me also. I learned about Christianity and how Christians should live their lives. I was delivered from the addiction to cell phones and evil companionships.

When I was small, I was sexually abused and that brought bad thoughts in me and I became addicted to bad thinking patterns without knowing about it. I started watching sexual internet pictures and pornography. Here God delivered me from that.

I had the practice of quarrelling with friends very often. I was an angry person. In my family it was a generational iniquity. My dad and his dad were very harsh and angry people. My dad was very rude with me and I became depressed. I was rejected and I began to behave harshly towards my parents. Here I confessed my sins which I had committed from a young age.

On the first day of the group training I had a fear of what would happen; what am I going to do and why am I here? My group was so loving and kind towards me. They helped in every way to be delivered. I confessed my sins and God delivered me. I forgave my parents and friends for how they had rejected me and I was delivered from the spirits of rejection. The hatred that I was having towards my dad and friends is gone. I really thank God for all these things.

In this prayer meeting, anger, brokenness and loneliness left me and I am fully delivered from everything that I was addicted to: phone, sexual thoughts and bad friends.

#88…Pouting Demon

We were getting close to doing a group deliverance session in the Transformation class when, out of the blue, a demon screamed out of a man, "We've been here for 4 generations. There are 7 of us and 5 have already been cast out. Why are you casting us out?" I always find it interesting that evil spirits don't have manners and will say the strangest things, not to mention that they can give us information that we can use against them!

The tone of voice was one of whining! The demon apparently was taken back that we would have the gall to disturb them and send them away!

You guessed it! The last two left shortly thereafter!

#89…White Wolf

Betty's ancestors were Native Americans. We didn't know much more about them. But near the end of our deliverance time with her, we said, "We command the demon in charge of all the other demons to give us your name. Give it now!" Out came a language I had never heard! I said, "No, you give it in English!" "White Wolf" was the answer. We didn't expect that! Then we found out that under it was squirrel, hawk, snake, owl, leopard and others! Her relatives had worshiped these animals and the spirits they had gotten from this false worship had been passed down to her and were more or less dormant.

Or were they? She said that, at times, she would find herself dancing in her room: strange dances similar to what we have seen Native Americans do.

Well, in the name of Jesus Christ we cast out many of these "animals!" Praise the Lord!

#90…Generational Sex Iniquity

My name is Christy Prince from Coimbatore.

I was born in a Roman Catholic family. I accepted Jesus in the year 1990.

I had a compulsive sexual drive from the age of 3 and was not able to overcome it.

When I came to this seminar, I came with alcohol addiction and was separated from my wife. Here I realized that I had rejection problem from the age of 8. The reason was that I was placed in a hostel for my studies and after my wife left me, I felt very lonely. It made me become an alcoholic. God delivered me from the spirits of rejection and filled me with the love of Christ.

The sexual drive was a generational iniquity. My grandparents owned Hindu temples and they were like a lord in Kerela and they had done atrocities to poor people and raped them. Now, God delivered me from the generational iniquity.

Now I am filled with great zeal for God and am going with joy to serve the Lord!

#91...From My Parents To Me

My life was covered with many evil spirits. I couldn't discern good from evil. I wanted to get delivered, but I couldn't. My father and mother are from temple priest families and I was under the attack of the enemy.

Here in this seminar, for the first 5 days, I was not co-operating with the teachings and there was no deliverance. But, when I was put in the ministry training groups at the beginning of the second week, my group members began digging into my history and I couldn't refuse to share with them. Finally, I found out that the problem I was facing was passed down my generational line. Then I confessed the sins of my forefathers and cut all the ungodly soul ties between myself and them. At that time, I felt something leave my head. I could feel the liberty in my mind and my mind became sound.

After that, when I looked at a girl, I didn't feel like looking at her in a sexy way.

Since my parents were from a temple priest family, I was attacked by negative fears. I was worried about my future. I confessed my sins and forgave my parents who were the cause of the negative fears. The spirit of fear manifested and came out through coughing and yawning. After the deliverance, all the negative fear was gone. (We would call this fear, anxiety) I felt boldness in my heart and I have faith in God that He will take care of my future. Praise the Lord for the wonderful healing. Thank you. God bless you.

#92...Family Gods

My name is S. Santhi from Erode.

When I came to this class, from the second day onwards, I began to receive deliverance from weakness and tiredness. When the teaching on anger was given, I could experience the deliverance from the spirits of anger, bitterness, rage and hatred. I give thanks to Jesus for what He did to me.

As the class was going on, I received deliverance from the spirits of asthma and allergy.

During the group training, many idol demons went away from me. The family gods that my parents had worshipped were having hold in me and I was delivered from the serpent spirit. Since I am not having children, I knew something happened in my womb during the deliverance; I felt pain in my stomach and demons leaving me. Generational curses were broken off of me.

I was suffering from asthma for about 40 years, and because of that I could not go through cold temperature. I had dust allergy and breathing trouble. I had to take the pills twice a day. But in this meeting God has delivered me and healed my asthma and allergy and infirmities. I feel free now.

#93...Generational Sex Addiction

My name is John David from Ariyalur.

I was in so much bondage when I came to this class. Because I work as a school teacher, I thought that it would be impossible to get leave for ten days to come to this class. However, I applied for the leave anyway. By God's grace, I got leave for the full 10 days.

I discovered that I had a number of generational bondages. My father had sexual addictions and the same addictions got a hold on me. But, God gave me deliverance from those problems while I was here.

Before coming here, I was severely tormented by witchcraft spirits. I often had pain in my right leg from them. Sometimes the pain was so severe that I considered cutting my leg off just to stop the pain. But, since I have been here, the Lord has healed me of that pain that came through witchcraft.

I also had been suffering with a cold for about 3 years when I arrived here. I was always sneezing and I had severe pain in my nose. Now I am completely free.

Also, when I was about 10 months old, my father left my mother and married another woman. Because of this, I suffered from rejection all my life. But, God has now healed me of that emotional wound. I also had an anger problem, fear, generational iniquities and idol spirits. I am truly free from all these problems now. Thank you very much.

#94...Family Curses Broken

My name is T. Tamizh Sindu from Thirunelveli.

I came to this meeting with a lot of confusion about my future, and I wanted to know what was going on inside me. I felt far away from God, though I could not specify any reasons. I wanted to serve God but didn't know how, and I could not find what God wants me to do. As I am working in a medical field, I thought it would be easy to reach out to people and proclaim the Gospel, but I was advised by others to do full time ministry and not to practice medicine. I really want to do full time ministry, but didn't know if it is what God wants me to do. I could not concentrate on anything due to this, and was emotionally weak, had fear, anger and self-blaming problems. I came to this meeting without informing my pastors, because they would not allow me to come if they knew that I planned to come.

I really thank God for all the ministries and the team members for all the love, support and encouragement they have given us. They actually listened to us, and were very friendly and accepting.

I thought that our family was a blessed family, and I never thought of curses in the family line. Here God revealed generational curses and also curses that I have brought into my life through my own sins. God broke the power of every curse and delivered me.

I learned about ungodly soul ties for the first time in this meeting. There were circumstances when I would repent for my sin and would forgive those involved in it, but I felt that I repeated the same type of sin again and again, the same sins I committed a long time back. Here I asked God to cut all ungodly soul ties between myself and the persons. Through that I received complete deliverance.

I had wounds of rejection inside me. The Lord helped me to find the different roots of rejection through the truth and healed those wounds. God also set me free from the defense mechanisms that I had chosen and the detrimental effects of rejection also.

God helped to find the roots of Anger and delivered me from spirits of anger.

I had self-condemnation. God delivered me and helped me to forgive myself.

I received great deliverance in the area of fear. Before coming to this meeting, I could not stand before a crowd because of fear. I had stage-fear, fear of men, and fear of rejection. Now I am freed from these fears.

Though I had received the Holy Spirit anointing before, yet I was confused because I was taught that shouting and screaming are the mighty power of God. I would actually blame myself for not screaming. God cleared those doubts and filled me with joy. I thank God for the teammates that He gave me for the training session the second week. In the team training I did cast out demons for the first time. Two members of our team accepted Jesus Christ as their personal Savior.

During the time of the Ministry of the Holy Spirit, I was comforted by the Holy Spirit and He filled my soul with joy and laughter. I really want to do this ministry. The pain the people had before was gone. Now, after the deliverance, the joy on their faces is awesome. My face is not the same as when I came here. Amen.

#95...Four Healed Of Many Things

My name is Aron Surbamaniam Ooty.

I attended the Inner Healing & Deliverance meeting at Coimbatore. I was born and brought up in a Hindu family. My wife also comes from a Hindu family. In 1973 we accepted Christ as our Lord and became Christians. I have one daughter and four sons.

This seminar we attended as a family, my daughter in law and granddaughter also came. My daughter in law was being tormented by evil spirits for about 10 years. She was tormented by a familiar spirit through a lady who was killed by an elephant attack. In this meeting she was delivered from that evil spirit. My granddaughter, Ilakkia, was suffering from stomach pain for about 7 and a half years. We have gone to so many hospitals. She even went through an operation for that stomach pain problem, yet she was still having pain. Every month we were taking her to the hospital for injections. Now she is delivered from that pain. We give glory to God. She was having anger and a fear problem and now God has delivered her from those problems also. My wife was suffering from diabetes for about 20 years. She had to take pills everyday and injections also. But the sugar level did not come to normal. We came here with full expectation that God will surely heal and deliver her. Now during the days of this meeting, she has had no need of taking the pills. God has healed her. She is normal now. No affect of diabetes is seen in her body.

In this camp, God has given us the baptism of the Holy Spirit for the first time.

My wife had anger problem. Now I see a great calmness in her. She also went through 2 operations for her stomach pain, and the pain was still there. Now she is healed from that pain.

For about 20 years I was suffering from diabetes, high blood pressure and an ulcer problem. My whole body was filled with sickness and the torment was increasing. Though we prayed, nothing happened. Sometimes I wanted to die because of the sickness. I also had a burning sensation in my chest and I was not able to eat well because of that.

Though I had become Christian, I was still lying, stealing, committing adultery, angry, jealous, prideful and had bribery problems in my life. I often spoke evil about others. I was worrying about not having enough money or our own house. In this meeting God has given deliverance from these problems. When I came to this meeting, on the first day, I could not write clearly because my right hand was shaking. But in the group ministry time when I confessed my sin of receiving bribes from others, I was delivered and now I am able to write clearly.

God has delivered us from traditional bondages and generational curses.

Another thing was that I suffered from asthma for 20 years. Once in every three months I had to go to the hospital to receive medicine for that. I was taking 12 pills three times a day daily. Now I am healed from that asthma. Now I am not taking any pills at all. I am able to eat and breathe normally.

We thank God for giving us healing and deliverance for all four of us.

For more stories of generational iniquity spirits and curses see #'s 24, 28, 33, 40, 46, 52, 65, 75, 104, 115, 137, 168.

Chapter 8
Spirits Of Infirmity

Demons can afflict a person's soul (mind) or body. When attacking the body, they are called spirits of infirmity. It is quite an awakening when one observes these spirits in people. Simply speaking, they make them hurt.

Near the end of His ministry, Jesus was teaching in a synagogue in Judea and a woman with such as spirit came in (Luke 13:10-17). She was bent over and had been that way for eighteen years. Jesus healed her and the spirit left.

How often we have seen people with infirmities that no medicine can help (Jeremiah 30:12-14)! They spend all that they have and get no relief (The doctors don't know what to do and won't admit it! After all, they are the doctors and are supposed to know all about body sicknesses!). When they confess their sins and iniquities, the spirits can be cast out and the problem goes away. This is what Psalm 103:3 says, "…who forgives all your sins and heals all your diseases…" Forgiveness first, then healing. In John 5, Jesus heals a man and then finds him later and says, "See, you have been made well. Sin no more lest a worse thing comes upon you." Sin and iniquities (perpetual sin) will cause spirits of infirmity to come in. Confession and repentance will allow them to be cast out.

When I was first learning about these spirits, they frustrated me. I would command a spirit out of someone's back and it would obey me but go into their head! Then I would command it out from there and it would go to their feet! One time I commanded the spirit out of a person's right leg that was bouncing up and down like a racecar piston and it immediately went to the left leg and did the same! I asked a deliverance veteran what to do and he said, "Isolate it." Then I would say, you will leave the [body part] and you will not go anywhere else but out of their body!"

#96…Leave My Mom

One of my high school students, Flora, who moved here from El Salvador, asked me one day if I could come pray for her mom because she was missing work from back pain. She worked in a factory and was on her feet a lot and the pain was so bad that she couldn't work. She would go to work feeling fine and when she arrived the pain in her back would not allow her to work. If something didn't change, she would lose her job and, being a single mother, it would be a real financial crisis for them.

When my wife and I arrived to their apartment, we pretty quickly determined that it was a spirit of infirmity in her lower back (She never had any trouble with her back except when she went to work.). We went through a series of prayers to "cut the roots" of demon entry and commanded the spirit out. It didn't budge.

In the past, we had already seen the effectiveness of people casting demons out of family members. They have more authority. I thought to ask Flora to join us (She was sitting quietly close by.). Now, this girl was a sweet little thing who never raised her voice about anything, ever. I thought, "No way! She won't even step on a bug on the sidewalk! She doesn't have the ability to cast out demons with powerful authority like we should do!" But, I've learned not to argue with God, so I said to her, "Put your finger right here [lower back by spine] and you command the spirit out." She did as I said and since mom didn't speak English, she spoke in Spanish and I understood it. What came out of her mouth still astounds me today, "You demon, come out of my mother! ***You are not allowed to be here anymore!! There are angels here to protect her and you must go! Go away now in the name of Jesus and don't ever come back!!***" Mom immediately coughed it out. I think she scared the demon away! My wife and I said nothing the whole time! We were in shock! I said, "Flora, where did *that* come from?!" She said, "I was in a world of peace and the words just came." Yes, and we know where those words came from: the Lord!

Several years later, Mom was still free! Glory to God!

#97…1.5 Arms

I was ready for church to start in Madurai, India, when I was informed that I was the preacher! I hadn't been told ahead of time so I had to "wing it" and come up with something on the spot. I didn't feel "anointed" in any way or "full of faith" or any such thing. In fact, I felt just the opposite. To my surprise, after I finished, a healing line formed and every single person in line was healed of something!

One of them was a man who could not lift his arm up. It could only go maybe half way and a pain in his shoulder would prevent it from going further. Doctors could not make it better either so for years he had to live with, shall we say, half an arm! I discerned that it was a spirit of infirmity in his shoulder so I commanded it out in the name of Jesus Christ and out it came and his arm shot straight up!

Two weeks later I was back in that church and asked for testimonies from the healings two weeks earlier. He spoke and raised his arm straight up again and said, "After years of not being able to, I can wash my hair in the shower now!" God is good!

#98...Intense Pain

This story is about a single father of three children (18, 16, and 15). The father is 38 years old. I met them when our church was knocking on doors and offering prayer for people. I had led a 15 year old kid to surrender his life to Christ. He went and got four of his friends to bring to us as we were still knocking on doors, offering prayer for people and sharing the Gospel. He really wanted his friends to meet us, and when he brought them up, I recognized a great opportunity to share the Gospel with all of them at once. Two of the children (of the father whom I'm about to share) were there, and the father noticed us and came over as well. No one else came to the Lord that day, but this is how I got to know this family.

The father and his three children began attending our church, which is very close to the apartments in which they live. So we were getting to know them. One of the weeks I went over to meet with the first 15 year old who'd given his life to Christ. I thought, "I need to go knock on the other kid's door and invite him to join us for Bible study." When I knocked on the door, the father was clearly having a really tough time. I asked if I could pray for him, and he proceeded to share some things going on in his life. For many, many months he'd been attempting to get help from the VA with some benefits and was really struggling. Just the day before, someone had given him the contact for a state senator who had helped them in a similar situation. He had made a call to this senator's secretary that morning. Then he had helped one of his neighbors move into a new apartment. While moving, the senator had gotten his message and decided to personally call him to find out what needs to happen and take care of it. Well, the father did not hear his phone ring and missed the call while he was helping his neighbor move. He attempted to call back, and the senator's secretary said something like, "I'm sorry, but since you missed his call he won't be able to help you directly now, but you can talk with me." In this father's mind, this would not be helpful now, and things would still not be resolved. He made a comment along the lines of "Every time I do something good, something bad always happens."

At some point in our conversation, the Lord opened a door for me to share the gospel with him. I had shared what Jesus said about how the Heavenly Father takes care of the birds of the air, the flowers of the field….but seek first His kingdom and His righteousness, and all these things will be added to you" (Matt 6:33). At this point in our conversation, the Lord had allowed me to see that this man was trusting in his own moral goodness in order to be accepted by God, and so I was explaining how we must transfer our trust away from ourselves, trusting in Jesus Christ alone to make us right with God. He was so close to giving his life to Christ, but he kept making comments like the previous one, "It seems like when I do something good, something bad will always happen." He had many examples of how this would play out in his life. (By the way, I think I still need to go through renouncing this specific lie in his life and applying the truth in Christ).

It was getting late, I needed to be somewhere, and I could see that he wasn't quite ready to fully trust in Jesus. So in my mind I'm kind of transitioning to leave when he said something about how he was experiencing darkness and "battling demons." I know some people will say they're battling demons and what they really mean is just some hard things are going on in their life, but I asked him to clarify what he meant about this. He went on to tell me how he had even "converted to Catholicism" in order to get deliverance from a priest, "but it didn't help. A fiery Pentecostal woman even prayed over me one time, but that didn't help either." I said, "Well, if you are experiencing anything demonic, I can command it to come out right now in the name of Jesus, and it must obey since I have the authority of Christ. Do you want me to do this?"

He said, "Yes." So I spoke out, "Any demons, I command you right now in the name of Jesus to come out." (Or "leave now" or something along those lines). I watched and nothing seemed to be happening. I asked if the darkness was still there, and he said that it was. I wasn't sure if there was, in fact, any demons involved. I had never done anything like this before, but I thought, "If I command any demons to manifest right now, they'll have to obey." So I said, "If there are any demons, I command you to manifest now in the name of Jesus." At this point, nothing seemed to happen. So I thought something like, "Well, I need to get going. I should probably attempt to pray over him, or something, and I can try to maybe get him connected to the counseling center at church or something."

He walked out on his apartment patio with me, and I'm looking for an opportunity to pray for him so I can leave when all of a sudden he cries out in pain, grabbing his chest. I'm like, "Whoa! What is going on, man!?" He was in a lot of agony, still gripping his chest, and he said something like, "I don't know… I've got so much chest pain…" I wasn't sure what was going on, but I knew God loves to heal people so I asked him if I could pray for him. He said yes. I usually ask people what the pain level is between 0-10 (so I can come back and test it after praying to see what God is doing). He said, still in agony, groaning and clutching his chest, "At least a-hundred…" I prayed a simple prayer of healing over him, and then asked him what the pain level was. Often when I pray this way God takes away the pain, and sometimes it lessens. There are times when the pain stays the same, but it never gets worse. At this time though, he said, "It's worse!"

At that moment, I realized this is how the demon is manifesting. I had commanded it to manifest, and it was now causing this excruciating pain in his chest. I also knew (I can't really explain how I knew this at the time, but I am pretty certain the Holy Spirit had revealed this to me in that moment) that he had been believing these lies (that "every time he does something good, something bad always happens"), and these lies were most certainly coming from a demonic source. I also knew in that moment, that as a consequence of the allegiance he had made with the demonic, this is why I couldn't merely cast out the demon(s) that were influencing him.

So I then knew that he needed to vocally renounce any and all agreement/allegiances he had made with the demonic before I could cast them out. I began telling him that he needs to say out loud, "I renounce all allegiances I have made with the demonic, in Jesus name." He couldn't say it! He wanted to say it, but couldn't get it out. For the next several hours we were in a spiritual battle where I was encouraging him to say this, and he battled to get it out. He couldn't even say the name of Jesus. In addition, the pain in his chest was still going strong. At times he would fall to his knees, still clutching his chest, groaning often with louder yells and groans here and there. I was praying over him, still seeking to get him to say it. At one point he held up his fist making a motion like he was massaging one of those little stress balls, and he said, "I feel like something is just doing this to my heart right now." By the way, based on what I know now, I wish I had commanded the demon to stop causing this pain, and it would have had to obey.

I knew the demon was lying to him because he'd be about to say it and then look at me and say something like, "I feel like if I say this something really bad is going to happen to the kids or something." I recognized this tactic of the demon, and so I was telling him, "If you want freedom, then you have to say it! The demon is lying to you. Don't listen to him." I knew he was an army veteran so I said something like, "Man, I'm telling you right now how to get out of this foxhole so we can get out of here, but you've got to take my hand and trust me. What I'm telling you is true! This is the way to freedom!" The demon was also causing some kind of brain fog and confusion as well because several times he had said things about how his mind seems so foggy as well.

He was on the verge of saying it at one point, and a car pulled in the parking lot right next to us while simultaneously a car alarm started going off in a nearby car. Then we had gone back inside and were sitting on his couch (still groaning in pain, clutching his chest). He was about to say it again when someone knocked on the door, interrupting us once again. There were several things that happened like this. At one point, he looked at me, recognizing this can't possibly be a coincidence, saying, "Mannnnn, you're not going to believe this, but I was about to say it again…"

It was about 6 or 7 on a Friday evening at this point, and I knew no one was over at the church so we could go there in order to have some uninterrupted space to try to get this thing out. So he walked his dog (still experiencing the chest pain), while I shot out a bunch of texts asking people to pray for this situation.

When we got to the church, we went straight up to the altar, getting on our knees. I was playing worship music from YouTube on my phone. By the way, earlier in his apartment I had been playing the Elevation Worship song that says, "What the enemy meant for evil, You turned it for good…You turned it for good." The pain really intensified when that lyric started.

As I was praying over him there at the front of the church, asking the Holy Spirit to help him it occurred to me to tell the demon to shut up! I said, "I command you to be quiet right now in the name of Jesus!" At this point, he was able to get out the statement. He was crouched down, head on his arm there on the raised platform. He was struggling so hard to say it, and so ever so slowly, as he was still groaning (there was also snot and tears at this point as he was forcing himself to verbalize it), he muttered, "I renounce….all….allegiance…..I've made……..with…the demonic…." I encouraged him to finish, "In the name of Jesus, man, in the name of Jesus!" He continued, "….in the name……of…Jesus……"

He looked up at me. "I feel like something shifted… something happened." "Did the demon leave?" I asked. "I don't know, but something definitely shifted."

I had received a text from a godly woman (the same one who had previously told me about renouncing) saying I should pray through the Lord's Prayer with him, specifically "deliver me from the evil one." My Bible was laying open right there in front of us where we knelt. I turned to Matthew 6 and led him through that prayer. I don't' remember exactly what I prayed, but there were some things the Holy Spirit led me to lead him in prayer as we went through that. When we got to the end I had him pray something along the lines of "Deliver me from the evil one right now, and clean me from all evil." After he prayed that the pain stopped. He looked up at me, and I could tell something was different.

I then encouraged him to pray and thank God. "I don't even know how to pray…I've tried to pray before, but I'm not even sure what to pray." God led me to open up to a psalm and use that to lead him in a prayer. His mind was still a bit fuzzy, but as I opened up to Psalm 34, reading through it and using that as a guide to pray, he prayed through it and I could tell his mind was clearing as we went through it. After praying through this he knew something was different. I hugged him for a bit. We had been through an intense battle.

"What if it comes back?" he asked. I explained to him that surrendering his life to Jesus and making Him the King of his life would allow him to be able to command anything to leave in the name of Jesus and it would have to leave. The Lord also led me to take him to Galatians 5 and talk about what it looks like to walk in the Spirit. Once I turned there, The Lord really highlighted Galatians 5:1 – "For freedom Christ has set us free, do not submit again therefore to a yoke of slavery". I realized that he had been in bondage for a long time. He hadn't experienced freedom in so long. The Lord brought an illustration to my mind that I'd heard before about elephants in captivity. The captors will often catch these elephants when they are very young and attach their legs by a small rope to a pole or something. When the elephants are young they can't get away from this tiny little pole. When they get big they are so used to standing there tied to the pole that they just stand there, and the captors don't even have to tie the rope to the pole. The elephants are so accustomed to being tied to the pole that they will just stand there with the rope around their leg. I told him this is kind of what it will be like for you now. You can walk in freedom, but you must consistently submit yourself to the Holy Spirit and walk in your freedom.

That same night we ended up having a Bible study with this father and two of his kids. The 18 year old surrendered his life to Christ that night, and both he and the father were baptized at our church on the same morning. I'm still meeting with them and helping them to grow closer to the Lord. He is doing much better, but I do I think a more thorough process of inner healing and deliverance would be really helpful for him.

One of his neighbors told me the next week after the initial deliverance that he wanted whatever James had. He said, "He is so different after whatever you did to him."

#99…Feet First

Thomas had been a Christian since he was young and was given the name of one of the Apostles by his Christian dad. Somewhere along the line he had become demonized and that's when I met him in India.

He had a spirit of infirmity and as we attempted to cast it out, it would move. It was in his back, then his feet, then his shoulder, then his head and so on. I asked Larry what to do about it and he said, "Isolate it". So, we told the spirit that it was only allowed to move out of the body and not to a different part. It ended up in Thomas' feet and did not move from there. I had him sit in front of me and put his feet in my lap and I put my hands around both shins and pulled them forward to the bottoms of his feet and commanded the demon out in Jesus' name. I did this for several minutes.

I got stares from people! A grown man, about twice the age of Thomas, with his hands on his legs, pulling them down to his dirty feet. Are we willing to do what needs to be done to get spirits out? Was he blessed that I was willing to humble myself and do what it took? Yes! I believe it was this love I showed him that eventually caused the spirit to leave.

The spirit left through his feet which is how it came in, in the first place. He had gone barefoot into a Hindu temple, years earlier, and by acknowledging this false God, the spirit came in.

#100…Christians With Demons?

Pastor Jonathan came to the Transformation Class in India kicking and screaming. His pastor friends had encouraged him to go in order to learn about deliverance so he could be more effective in his service for the Lord. But, he was certain that, "Christians can't have demons." Boy, was he in for a surprise!

He had, for a long time, suffered with pain in his right leg. The doctors didn't know what to do so he just endured it. Whenever he walked, he hurt. Then, during one of the ministry sessions, an evil spirit came out of his leg and he was healed! He felt it leave and could not deny that he had been tormented by a spirit of infirmity. His leg was totally and instantly healed, in the name of Jesus Christ, when the demon left!

How ironic it is that now Pastor Jonathan is one of the great deliverance ministers in all of India! He travels from church to church watching the Lord set Christians free as he casts evil spirits out of them! I guess you can now say that, yes, he knows that Christians can have demons!

#101…Knife In Stomach

As I ministered to Johnny, I "saw" a knife in his stomach. I said, "Knife in the stomach, in the name of Jesus, come out!" What else could I do? I've seen stranger things when ministering. After many months of suffering with stomach pain and not being able to eat much, he was healed. The spirit of infirmity had come out.

About a year later, he told me that he had not had any trouble with his stomach since the "knife" came out! Praise the Lord!

#102…Menstruation And Digestion Problems

My name is G. Salomi.
I came from Hindu traditional family. I have received Jesus as

my savior and I got baptized. Yet I had problems in my behavior. When meeting people, I struggled in respecting them and in obedience also. I was thinking that I attracted only Jesus and so I am facing obstacles and failures. But God clearly told me that He had chosen me for His purpose. I was trusting Jesus in the 15 years of my spiritual journey but I doubted God many times when I faced challenges due to the lack of faith in God though He had done miracles in my life.

In this class, God has healed me of digestion problem and menstruation cycle problem completely. All glory to God.

I was a stubborn person in the area of receiving God's Word. I used to receive God's Word partially but I chose my own way even when I meditated on the Word. I was fed up with many things. When I came to this class, after the first week, the stubbornness has gone from me. While the transformation processes were going on, God revealed His purpose of choosing me. I repented of my own ways and He started showing His plan about my life.

In the second week, I was nervous during the ministry training time. I was thinking that I can't do what all these people are doing. I was stubborn and was not fully participating in the deliverance sessions. But God helped me to understand each and every demonic power, when it will affect the people, and how to overcome the satanic activities one by one by finding and removing the roots. The teaching manual with detailed explanation and practical training helped me for my spiritual eyes to be opened. I learned the truth to set the captives free. I am freed from spiritual blindness and stubbornness. Glory to God!

#103…Back Pain Gone

This weekend of deliverance was such a relief to finally get rid of the feelings and emotions of guilt and shame from my past. It was one thing to know I am forgiven and redeemed, but another to physically feel relief from burdens I had been carrying for years.

I am grateful for my team (Karen and Shawn) for their persistence and thoroughness and willingness to give of themselves so I might achieve complete freedom and no longer be influenced by spirits of emotional pain, bitterness or critical thinking. I have learned much and feel I can better be used by God in the future.

I no longer fear to be able to provide for my daughter. I know and believe that I am a good mom and I make good decisions for her care and that God is fully in control.

Thank you to everyone on the deliverance/freedom team who make these weekends possible.

Additionally, my back pain no longer torments me and feels better than it has in over a year. I am so grateful for this relief! God is truly amazing and I love Him so much.

I am excited to experience a close walk with Him now that I am completely free!

#104…Asthma Healed

My name is Chithra Saagar from Hosur.

My husband and I were both Hindus. I was born and brought up in a Brahmin family.

Even though I have been a Christian for 17 years, I had not yet been healed of asthma. I suffered from asthma from the age of 6 months. Many times I almost died. More than 35 times I struggled with this bondage. Through the Inner Healing and Deliverance ministry I was completely healed and delivered.

My husband and I were constantly quarreling because both of us came from a Hindu background. We had so many curses on our lives. Many times we prayed and fasted, but saw no change in our problems. Outwardly, we looked like a very good Christian couple, but at home we were continuously fighting, misunderstanding one another and being stubborn. I was also tormented by fear about our children's future.

Finally, my husband and I decided to get a divorce. Just as we were going to do it, one of our friends told us about an Inner Healing seminar that he attended. He then helped my husband to attend the last seminar in Salem, where he received great deliverance. When my husband came home from the Salem class, he was like a new person. All the old things had passed away from him. After that, I came to this Dharmapuri seminar and was delivered from bondages and curses.

I had deep rejection wounds and was healed. I also received deliverance from a generational curse of divorce. During the ministry of the Holy Spirit, He comforted me and filled me in a special way.

I thank God for the healing and deliverance he gave to us.

#105…Excruciating Pain

My name is Cindy Hawkins.

I had back pain for over ten years. I felt excruciating pain daily.

I had rehab and even surgery which only seemed to make it worse. I am PAIN FREE for the first time in so long.

I felt so oppressed and heavy before starting deliverance. Almost weekly I was feeling that I was worthless: not worth God's love or life itself. My heavy oppression is gone! I have hope and feel like myself for the first time in so many years. Praise God!

#106…Many Physical Problems

My name is G. Gurupaul.

Before I came to this meeting, I was suffering from headaches and heaviness. Because of that, my personal everyday life activities were heavily affected. I was not able to focus on doing things. That was a painful problem. Last year my wife attended this meeting. When she came back home, she shared all the wonderful things God was doing. God had mercy on me and helped me to attend the meeting this year. In each teaching, God began to speak to me, and when I committed my heart to the Word of God, I received Him into my heart. The bondages of Satan in my life were broken.

I received great deliverance and healing to my physical body also. When we had the team training, I received more healing and deliverances, especially my headaches which are now gone and I am delivered. Every teaching of this meeting brought transformation into my life. I thank everyone who taught us the teachings. Through these teachings my soul was strengthened. Really, this is an awesome meeting. All glory to God. Let His Name be glorified.

#107…Yoga

My name is Abilash from Nagercoil.

I have been working in Chennai for a year now. This is my third time taking this seminar. I was suffering from joint pain that went from my leg up into the back of my hip. The pain was so bad that I could not live in a place where the weather was very cold. Somehow I made up my mind to come to this Transformation seminar. On the third day, the teaching on healing through forgiveness was given and I was very attentive. I asked forgiveness from God for holding bitterness and unforgiveness towards some people. Immediately the joint pain was completely gone. It was a supernatural physical healing. Now there is no pain in my leg and hip. Praise the Lord for the healing.

On the 7th day of the seminar, I was delivered from the spirit of Yoga. It is also known as the spirit of Amirtha, a lady who calls herself as God. She used to deceive people so they could see Jesus in her. This is an antichrist spirit. Praise the Lord for delivering me from such an evil spirit.

On the 8th day, I got delivered from a serpent spirit. It had deceived me for a long time and by the grace of God it was cast out.

On the 9th day, during the group training, I confessed my sins of rebellion, picking fights and quarreling with others. The demons came out through my hands and legs.

On the last day, the teaching on brokenness and the Ministry of the Holy Spirit was very much a blessing for me. God, through the Holy Spirit, bound up my wounds and I felt comforted inside.

Praise the Lord for bringing daddy and his team all the way from USA to be a blessing for me. May God bless him more and more and extend his boundaries. This ministry is needed in India for the last days.

#108…Spirit Of Pain

My name is Lalitha from Chennai.

For many years I was suffering from stomach, leg and hand pain. It was greatly disturbing my daily routine. I couldn't do anything.

I was bound by demons because of my idol worship. Here in this seminar, I confessed my idol worship and repented and the spirit of pain left me totally. Praise the Lord! Now there is no pain in my body and I can do my daily work. Thank you very much for the inner healing team. God bless you!

#109…Chronic Headache

My name is G. Gurupaul from Chennai.

Before I came to this meeting, I was suffering from a headache and heaviness in my heart. Because of that, my personal everyday activities were affected. I was not able to focus on doing things. It was a painful problem.

Last year my wife attended this meeting. When she came back home, she shared all the wonderful things God was doing in the class. God had mercy on me and helped me to attend the meeting this year.

During this meeting, in each teaching, God began to speak to me, and when I committed my heart to the Word of God and received it into my heart, the bondages of Satan in my life began to be broken. I received great deliverance as well as healing to my physical body. During the team training, the second week, I received more healing and deliverances. Especially, my headache is gone. Every teaching of this meeting brought transformation in my life. I thank everyone who taught. Through these teachings my soul has been strengthened. Really, this is an awesome meeting. All glory to God. Let His name be glorified.

#110...Nerve Spasms

My name is Karen Hammond.

For 20+ years I have had a very unusual illness, which my mother and grandmother both had, and no physicians have been able to determine the cause. We have, what I call nerve spasms, which cause intense sharp pain and triggers muscle spasms in our shins, calves, thighs, feet, and arms all at the same time, therefore it crazy awful painful. The pain is so excruciating we pass out from it. We have all had numerous tests done, it's not an imbalance of electrolytes such as magnesium, potassium, calcium, additionally nerve studies, x rays nothing…nothing can be found and there have been no solutions! NO answers! I finally asked my physician if it could be "an infirmity for which there is no medicine to heal" (Jeremiah 30:13). My physician is a Christian and his response is "maybe." I've commanded spirits off, had healing, deliverance, anointing oil…still nothing.

One day in my personal devotions this came to mind… manipulating, controlling, legalism, rigidness, religious spirits, pride, denominationalism, unbending, etc…..I knew what it meant! I grew up in a very legalistic environment, my grandfather was a pastor in this particular denomination, my mother was raised in it and she was very affected by it and my dad was a pastor in this denomination. I went to the Christian college associated with it…I knew from my devotions that morning that those spirits were associated with our illness so I started calling them out …"in the name of Jesus; control, legalism, rigidness, manipulation, unbending, pride, denominational control in the name of Jesus to leave me!!!!" I prayed to forgive those in my life, grandfather, religious leaders, family members who brought the rigidness, legalism, manipulation, unbending, pride and denominational control into my life and I broke ungodly soul ties with those individuals.

I later called my mother, who is in her 90's, with this revelation and she felt I was correct and she started calling them out also. I have not had any of those severe pains/spasms since that day; I thank Jesus for setting me free and for regaining my health in this area! All praise, honor, and glory go to Him...Praise Him for removing this spirit of infirmity!

I also thank God for bringing my husband and me into the knowledge of how Jesus came to set the captive free, and teaching us and growing us in that so we can not only claim it for ourselves, but also for others.

For more stories that include spirits of infirmity see #'s 1, 25, 39, 46, 50, 52, 58, 62, 63, 92, 95, 135, 138, 165.

Chapter 9
Casting Out by the Spoken Word

I've been a Christian believer for close to 50 years and if there is one thing I've noticed that believers don't "get," it is the power of the spoken Word of God. The sword of the spirit is the only offensive weapon in the armor of God (Ephesians 6:17: "Word" is *rhema* in the Greek which is spoken words.). When the Word of God is spoken, mighty angels go into action (Psalm 103:20). Throughout the Gospels and Acts, miracles, including the casting out of evil spirits, follow the teaching of the Word. Faith is built by hearing *rhema* words (Romans 10:17).

Demons hate hearing God's Word! A good example is the very first time I cast a demon out of someone. Hey, it is the first story below!

#111…Giant Ice Cube

Linda lived in Monroe, NY, and had a number of evil spirits inside of her. She became a Christian and then needed deliverance. She lived with her mother who practiced various occultist things in her home including séances. Included in the home were various artifacts of pagan gods that Linda and her mother had brought back from Greece. Although I was never in her home, I was told by others who had been there that the presence of evil was noticeable and that they even felt invisible hands on their throats.

Linda's deliverance was in stages. We were truly novices; we had no idea what we were doing but we loved her and desired to see her delivered. The first demon was cast out by my friend, Bill, when he was at her home. It put up a fight and he fumbled around a bit but I was told that when it finally left she was very much better and full of God's peace. Bill did not even know there were more demons in her but kept me in the loop just in case. I had not met her until later but did speak to her on the phone. She told me to stay away unless I knew what I was doing because this was **real** and she did not want anyone getting involved who could be caught off guard. In her mind this was a life and death thing and if demons surfaced again she did not want anyone killed. I assured her that I was aware of what was going on and could handle something if it came up (Where did I get the courage to say that?! I really did not know what I was doing but I was willing to do whatever it took if needed. Of course, I did not know at the time that demons could not harm me.).

It was a cold December evening in 1985. There was a knock at my front door and when I answered it the woman said, "Hi, I'm Linda!" She apologized for coming over without notice but she had been praying and reading her Bible and another demon had surfaced that was threatening to kill her if she didn't stop so she said she knew she had to get over to my home and get help. As I stood there I did not know what to do with her or how she figured out where I lived but I knew enough to know that God is able to help in time of need so before fear could grab hold of me I said, "Well God bless you. Come on in!" We got acquainted and put on a pot of coffee (Yes, coffee was still brewed back then!).

Pretty soon we were sitting with our coffee and I silently asked God, "What do I do now?" Immediately the answer came, "Get your Bible." So I went to the other room and brought it back. As I began to open it I heard, "Romans 8." So I turned to Romans chapter 8 and began to read, "There is therefore now no condemnation to those who are in Christ Jesus..." As I did this, Linda began to fidget. I continued to read on and on, "...But if the Spirit of Him who raised Jesus from the dead dwells in you, He who raised Christ from the dead will also give life to your mortal bodies through His spirit who dwells in you..." About this time Linda said, "Feel my hand." I did and it was ice cold...like it had just come out of the freezer. She was tensing up as well and fidgeting more. I kept reading on, "...For as many as are led by the Spirit of God, these are the sons of God..." Her demon, which identified itself as Antonio, started to tell her things to tell me. Linda said, "I think I need to go so that I don't leave this thing with you." I said, "You're not leaving until its gone!" I did not know how it was going to play out but I was committed to see it through.

Things progressed rather quickly from this point on. I continued reading from Romans 8, "...What then shall we say to these things? If God be for us who can be against us..." Linda said, "He wants you to know you don't have as much power as you think you do." I responded to her and then kept reading as her discomfort was even more apparent,

"That's what he wants me to think so I won't use it against him……
…"Who shall separate us from the love of Christ? Shall tribulation or distress, or nakedness or persecution…" Suddenly I was interrupted and words came out of Linda's mouth but were in a different voice, "We've heard that before!" I looked up startled and Linda had the most bazaar expression on her face. I can only describe it like a clown's face…strange…not natural. I reacted, "What?" Immediately "Antonio" obeyed me and said the exact same thing the exact same way, "We've heard that before!" This demon, like all demons, could not stand to hear the Word of God. They will listen to sports or politics or whatever else you want to tell them but when the Word of God, that which is alive and powerful and sharper than any two-edged sword (Hebrews 4:12), is spoken to them they simply cannot stand it.

Linda began to cry uncontrollably. The Lord said, "Hold her!" I grabbed on and held her tightly. It felt like I was holding a giant ice cube that was shaking. I did not know what to do except pray so, silently, I said, "God, get rid of this thing in the name of Jesus Christ." The moment I silently said the word "Christ," I felt a tingle at the bottom of my spine. Over about a ten second time period of time, as Linda cried and shook, it moved up my spine and when it reached the top of my head, I felt the demon leave her body. She was instantly warm, limp and completely at peace! **WOW**! She stopped crying and said, "It's gone." I said, "I know." Within a few minutes she was on her way home, free of "Antonio" forever!

I can hardly describe the joy I felt over helping Linda. I did not have a Bible degree. I was not a pastor of a church. I was just a believer trying to make a difference. For God to allow me to be a part of her deliverance just blew my mind. This is one reason why I say that you don't have to be an Apostle Paul to cast out demons. If you are a Christian, you meet the requirements! You have Christ in you and that includes the power and authority to do the job. The question is; are you willing?

Over the next several weeks, five or six more demons were cast out of Linda. I was not involved in them but I know that each encounter was different. We cannot put God in a box. He will choreograph each encounter if we are faithful.

I don't remember the exact details but I know that Bill was with her when the last one came out. She was outside and walking in circles in the snow in bare feet! Bill said, "Do it!" By this time she knew the routine and what to do so ***she*** said out loud, "In the name of Jesus Christ, ***leave!***" It left!

#112…Christ In You

Meghan had demons. I knew that but I didn't know how to cast them out yet.

We were in a meeting and the preacher was teaching with authority. I sat behind her so I could observe and learn. When he got to Colossians 1:27, he boldly said, "It's Christ in you! Christ in ***you***! ***Christ…in…you, the hope of glory***!" Every time he said, "Christ," she moved backward in her chair like there was an unseen force pushing her.

Finally, the demon in her could not stand it any longer and forced her out of the room, walking on all four's like an animal! I can only describe that she looked like a giant beetle. She went to the kitchen where the leader took her outside and cast it out of her! WOW!

#113…Bathroom Screaming

I was teaching Bible study in church when Stephanie walked out. It was not unusual for this to happen as people sometimes need to use the restroom. However, moments later, we heard blood curdling screams. My wife and I both recognized this as not natural, but demonic: something we've heard before. So we left the room and went looking for the source. We found Stephanie screaming in the women's room. We immediately went in and began to cast the spirits out as the screaming continued. Two more deliverance team members joined us and then a security person and a church pastor came in (Someone from another Bible study heard the screaming and called for help.). When the security person and pastor saw that it was us, they basically said, "Oh, they are casting our spirits…no problem." And they left.

We returned to Bible study after casting the demons out and one of the attendees, who was there for the first time, got saved right then and there, having seen the power of God. Praise the Lord!

What is the lesson here? When the Word of God is taught with boldness, evil spirits will react; they hate the Word of God!

#114…No!!

I was teaching the Word of God and talking about how important words out of our mouths are from Mark 11:23 and Ephesians 6:17. Julia was near the front and began to speak (For years she had been a "Negative Nancy" and always talked bad about her husband and what a bad wife she was and what a bad marriage they had and oh pitiful her!). She was going to say something like, "Oh but Pastor, my marriage is so bad..." Speaking by the Spirit of God, I cut in boldly and loudly. Here's what happened, "Oh Pastor, my marriage…" *"is going to be awesome!"* Immediately the demon screamed out of her mouth, "Nooooo!" I said, "Yes, and you are about to leave!" Some deliverance team members went to her side and finished casting the evil spirit out of her.

She received great deliverance and now when I see her, she says, "I'm a great wife and I have a great marriage!" She is and does too!

#115…Angry Fist

My name is Nancy Blatnik.

When my husband and I were first married, I dealt with an anger problem--mainly directed towards him, but also towards others as well. The least little thing could set me off and I would feel no control whatsoever over it. I could feel it coming on but before I could check it, I would lash out in a physical attack against him. I was a 95-pound weakling and he was a strong 6-foot young man, but I do recall punching him pretty hard numerous times. Thankfully, he never reciprocated. When I expressed this anger towards others it was not done physically like it was against him. About five years into our marriage we were working at a Christian camp as counselors and he said something that set me off. As I went to reach out my fist on this occasion, the Lord stopped me and said (almost audibly, at least to me): *"You have a spirit of anger."*

This stopped me in my tracks, for I had never even considered such a thing. I don't even think that at the time I believed a Christian could have a demon at all inside of them. We lived in a cabin with several students and had our own private suite, so instead of hitting him, I went into our room to consider what I had just heard from the Lord. When I asked Him about it, He told me that it had been passed down to me from my mother. This made perfect sense to me because she could flare up in a heartbeat and come after my brother and me for the least little thing. We were terrified of her. A lot of her anger was aimed at men, probably because she grew up with an abusive father; and I believe this is why mine was so much more intense towards my husband than it was towards others.

I then asked the Lord what I should do and He gave me clear instructions. He told me to turn in my Bible to Ephesians 4:31 - 32, which says, "Let all bitterness, wrath, anger, clamor, and evil speaking be put away from you, with all malice. And be kind to one another, tenderhearted, forgiving one another, just as God in Christ also forgave you." He told me to read it aloud and when I did, I was deeply convicted, especially when I reached the end section where it said to forgive one another just as God in Christ had forgiven me. Wow. I was cut to the heart and I wept.

But He didn't stop there. He told me to memorize these Scriptures and to say them as soon as I felt that anger beginning to build in me. I was not good at memorizing Scriptures at the time, but I was determined to overcome this horrible thing in my life that made me strike out at the man I loved and at others. And I was also horrified at the thought of having a demon inside me and wanted to be rid of it.

The first time after this that I felt that anger beginning to rise in me, I immediately started saying the verses. I had them down--they were embedded within my mind--and so it was easy to spit them out. I had to go all the way through the two verses, and at first it was always the last part (forgiving others as I had been forgiven) that was the clincher that would "talk down" that damnable spirit. I could literally feel a fight inside of me as if there were two beings within me--the demon and the Christ inside of me.

After probably the first three incidents where it was necessary to use these scriptures to calm myself, I started realizing that the quelling of this demon was happening sooner, rather than at the end of the verses. After a few more times, it finally came to the point that I was barely uttering "Let all bitterness..." before there was quietness in my soul. It was as if the demon was entirely gone! (This happened within a time period of two or three weeks.)

At that point I asked the Lord outright, "Is it gone?" He answered me clearly, "Yes my child. But you must always remember those scriptures and use them to guard your heart, for you will be tempted again."

Although it's true that I have been tempted with anger since then, it is not at all as it used to be. First of all, through the years it has become more and more rare for me to even experience that temptation; secondly, when I have been tempted, it has never been with the uncontrollable urge that I had before He delivered me. And over the past couple of years, He has also been teaching me a lot about humility which has helped to produce much more patience within me.

I am so grateful to Him for loving me enough to speak to me and coach me through my deliverance. I'm aware that deliverance may not always happen this way, but I guess He knew that I would hear Him and receive mine in this manner.

He sent His word and healed them, And delivered them from their destructions. --Psalm 107:20

#116...I Couldn't Stand It

Debbie was tormented with nightmares in which she would be hanging by her fingertips and the fires of hell were below her, ready to burn her up. These nightmares had gone on for years. Obviously, they were terrible! She came to us for deliverance and her husband, Jack, joined us.

After gathering information, we began the ministry. When the demon surfaced, it had her wag her finger at her husband and it said, "No!" several times. Jack had not taken part in anything like this and wasn't even sure he believed in it, but he did his part anyway. He believed in the power of the spoken Word, so he picked up his Bible and started reading it out loud. The evil spirit became even more annoyed and soon thereafter it exited Debbie. Glory to God!

Afterwards, Debbie told us that she (really, the demon) hated when we spoke the Word to her, but she hated it even more when Jack did (family members have more authority). The Word of God is alive, powerful, and sharp (Hebrews 4:12)! "If you can't stand the heat, get out of the fire!" The demon couldn't stand the "heat" of the Word of God and left!

#117...Speaking In Tongues

Just when you think you have seen everything, along comes something new! This was the case in 2022 during a Freedom Weekend deliverance.

We had about an hour left with Becky's deliverance as the spirits were coming out readily do to the teaching of the Word, confession/repentance and forgiveness. We were "between" demons when one of them spoke through her and said, "Will you tell him to stop talking?" In the distance, in another room, I could hear someone talking very faintly. Becky later told me it sounded like he was yelling in her ear.

I left to find out who was talking and found out it was Frank, the husband of one of the team members, who had come to pick up his wife thinking that she would be about done. I asked, "Are you speaking in tongues?" He answered, "Yes." I said, "The demon doesn't like it. Keep doing it." I motioned for Frank to come closer to our room. As he did, the evil spirit became more animated and insistent, "Tell him to stop! He's hurting my head!"

He kept getting closer and louder and louder with tongues until he was right next to Becky. Finally, the demon screamed, "***Shut uuuuuuuup!!***" Then it left!

I don't know what Frank was saying in tongues, but it was from God and was certainly hitting the mark!

I asked him to stay with us and he continued to speak in tongues and the spirits, one by one, voiced their displeasure before they came out!

In hindsight, I think bigger, stronger demons were now coming out and we needed more "heavy artillery" to get them out! God provided all that we needed and Becky was set free!

#118…Mean To Her Husband

I was studying the Word of God and learning about how to cast out demons. It seems as though the Lord would put me in situations that I had just enough knowledge to help those who were demonized. Such was the case in Nashville, TN in 1994.

My customer, Sharon, knew about my desire to help those who are demonized and she told me one day about her situation. She was about 30 years old and a great Christian along with her husband. She said, "Sometimes I am so mean to Don (husband)! The other day he said to me, 'I want my wife back.' And I said, 'She's not here anymore!' I couldn't believe I said that!" She agreed with me that it wasn't her that said it. She arranged for me to meet with her and Don for lunch and talk about how to get her free.

When we met, I remember the look of desperation in their eyes! They attended a church that didn't believe Christians could have demons so they couldn't go for help from the pastors there. In their minds, I was their only hope. Boy, did I feel awkward! I admitted that I was still learning, but the one thing I knew was that demons hate the

Word of God and I shared a story about how I had helped someone get free simply by reading the Bible out loud to her.

A few days later, I saw Sharon, "You won't believe what happened! I was being ***so mean*** to him and he opened up his Bible and started reading it out loud to me. I ***hated*** it! He kept reading and then I felt the demon leave through my feet. I've been fine ever since!" Later, Don told me, "I didn't even know what I was reading. I just opened my Bible and read." The Word of God is alive, powerful and sharp (Hebrews 4:12)! To God be the glory!

About two years later was the last time I saw them and Sharon was still free…no issues at all with evil spirits!

#119…Leaven And Lump

I was ministering in India to Andrew, a Christian name he had been given when he converted from Hinduism. He was manifesting a demon and we didn't know what it was. Earlier, he had told us that he knew he had some sort of Hindu god spirit in him but didn't know what it was. Through my translator, we asked its name. It gave a Hindu name. I said, "No, what kind of spirit are you?" It gave the answer in the Tamil language translated to "Serpent."

We told Andrew to come back and within moments we were talking to him. We told him he had a serpent spirit and asked how he got it. He then remembered going into the temple years earlier. He repented of this sin and forgave all those who had been involved in getting him to worship it.

We then commanded the spirit out. It manifested by his hands coming together in front of him, something we see a lot with serpent spirits, especially in India. It was stubborn and wouldn't come out so I asked, "Lord, what do we do?" He said, "Bible." I grabbed it.
"I Corinthians 5:7." After reading it, I said, "In the name of Jesus Christ, old leaven, go out; new lump, come in." At that moment the demon left! Why? I don't know, but the Lord does and by following His directive, the man was set free. WOW!

Chapter 10
Casting Demons Off People

When I was studying the Word of God as I was preparing my first book, *Ekballo: What the Bible Teaches About Every Christian's Authority Over the Evil Spirit Realm*, I noticed that when Jesus cast out the demons in the first record, recorded in Mark 1 and Luke 4, the English is the same, "Be quiet and come out of him." However, in Mark, "out of" is the Greek preposition *ek* (out of) while in Luke it is *apo* (away from). Jesus would have been speaking Aramaic so whatever he said would include both. So, Jesus cast spirits out of and away from the person. As one studies the other records in the Gospels, *ek* and *apo* are both seen over and over again. So, casting demons away from, or off of people, is part of the authority He has given us.

Many times, as you will read below, people can feel overwhelming sadness, depression, sexual tension, fear, anger or other things that are out of the ordinary. Yes, the demons could be in the person, but they can also be on them and can be gotten rid of quickly by simply commanding them to leave. "You spirit of fear, leave me now!" could be an appropriate command. If the sensation goes, you know what it was.

How subtle it can be! We must always be wary that we do not wrestle against flesh and blood, but against spiritual entities (Ephesians 6:12).

#120...Unwelcome Breakfast Guest

My name is Bob Hammond.

For several months I had been preparing to teach in the Transformation Class in Salem, India. There would be about 100 people there seeking deliverance and transformation for their lives and I was anticipating many people being set free from demons in Jesus' name.

It was the morning of the first day which is normally filled with excitement and expectation that God would show up. As I ate breakfast with two other Americans, this is what went through my mind, "Why am I here? [Sigh] Do I have to teach? [Sigh] I miss my wife. [Sigh] I want to go home. [Sigh]" One of the team members said, "Bob, are you OK?" "No, I feel sad." And then I said to the other American, "Will you pray for me after breakfast?" Without hesitating he said, "In the name of Jesus, **GO**!" Within moments I was glad I was there; I was ready to teach and I didn't want to catch the next flight home to see my wife! He said, "You had a spirit of depression on you." This was the first time I had experienced such a thing. I had seen it in the Word of God (casting spirits away from people instead of out of people), but had not done it or been freed myself.

The class was awesome and many were set free, in Jesus' name, from demons. The spirit of depression never returned! Glory to God!

#121...Depression Go

Depression is an interesting topic to me. If you ask ten people for their opinions about it, you will probably get ten different answers. One thing I know is that depression can be, and most of the time is, an evil spirit. It can get in someone or on someone. If it gets in, it takes more work to get it out, and if it gets on, it will go easily in Jesus' name.

A bunch of us were at a convention in Pittsburgh and we were asked to minister in a church on Sunday morning, the day before we were to leave to go home. When I knocked on the hotel room door to remind my friends that it was time to get going, Jack opened the door and I could see his wife Jill, sitting up in bed, who said, "You go along without me. I just want to get home." I have never known Jill to turn down a ministry opportunity and I could tell she wasn't right. So I said to Jack, "You can do what you want, but if I were you, I'd cast that spirit of depression off of her."

Next thing I knew, we were all off to minister...including Jill! I asked what happened and Jack said, "I cast the spirit off of her." and she said, "It's gone and I'm fine!" God is good and he has given us authority over demons!

#122...Demons Try To Return

I finally got to go back to one of my favorite places, Sierra Leone, Africa, to see all my kids and friends. But this trip brought sickness, prayer, and spiritual warfare.

If you know my story, I will wear that suffering with a badge of honor as I like to be part of the "God saved my life" club. I told God I would never stop sharing that story.

Something that came out of that experience was trauma, fear and anxiety. Ever since that happened, I cannot watch a hospital scene in a show or movie without crying, like really crying. Also, if someone I know gets sick, anxiety will pop up and rear its ugly head and all the thoughts start rushing in about this person dying. I get aggravated at myself when these thought come to mind because I know how to trust God…He saved my life!!!

For the last four years, this is a struggle I have had that I did not experience prior to my malaria scare. I have chalked it up to PTSD, but part of me wanted to be reminded of this experience as it strengthened my faith. But when it happens (fear, anxiety), it can be debilitating.

The night before we were leaving for Africa, the anxiety started creeping in, reminding me of what could happen if I go. What if I get malaria again? What if someone gets sick? It was actually making me sick thinking about it! I called my good friend in the wee hours of the morning, and she was encouraging me to go. She kept telling me God uses us there and Satan is just trying to prevent us from doing the work of God. She even said, "You may suffer the whole time you're there, but God calls us to suffer. Look at Paul!" I will be honest…I was annoyed with what she was saying. Why would I say yes to suffering?

That morning, it was beautiful out and my husband said, "Let's go for a walk." We needed to decide if I was going or not, because my mind was screaming, "STAY HOME!" On that walk, God met me and spoke to me. He told me that those of us who follow Christ WILL suffer. It's not optional. But what I needed to remember was Christ suffered for me on a cross dying a horrible death. Feeling anxious, nauseous and uncomfortable is the least I could do for a Holy God who suffered for me. I want to be more like Paul, who knew exactly what he was getting in to when he said yes to Jesus, and he went anyway. I want to learn how to suffer well.

So, on the plane I went. The trip there was rather uneventful. Lots of hours sitting on the planes or in airports, but we finally made it there the next evening. I felt fine the first night…slept like a baby and felt fine the next day (Saturday) when we reunited with all those beautiful faces I have grown to love. But Sunday brought sickness. I was having a lot of nausea and headaches and just not feeling well. I ended up staying back as the rest of the team went to church to experience what I think is an awesome church experience.

Monday morning our team was expected to leave around 8:30 am to head to a village that we hadn't visited before. A baby church had been planted there about a year and a half ago, so these people are new to the Gospel. I was so excited to go and meet the pastor and his wife, but I woke up feeling awful. This caused my anxiety to be at an all-time high, along with feeling extremely nauseous. I couldn't tell If I was sick because of something physically wrong with me (did I have malaria again?), or just mentally messed up.

What do you do when you feel this bad? Call in prayer warriors to pray over you – and we had lots on our team! A wonderful teammate named Ashlyn sat next to me and asked me lots of questions. A little background on Ashlyn – she received a dream from God a year ago that she would be going to Africa and perform healing miracles. Here she is in Africa. I think maybe the first miracle she performed was on me. She taught me that the fear I was having was a sin…something I have never thought of before. Fear is your lack of trust in God. Fear is a liar and is from Satan. She told me to repent of that sin, which I eagerly did. But, for clarification, not all fear is sin…there is some legitimate fear that doesn't cause you to sin. If we allow our fear to control us, rather than trust in God, this leads to sin. For God has not given us the spirit of fear, but of power and of love and of a sound mind. – 2 Timothy 1:7.

Next, she told me that anxiety, fear and trauma may be unclean spirits that need to be cast out. Those things are not of God – they are tools Satan uses to prevent you from doing the will of God. She taught me how to pray, rebuking fear, trauma and anxiety using the mighty name of Jesus…OUT LOUD! I don't typically pray like this, so it was new to me, but I wanted to get rid of these things tormenting me and I followed her directions to a T. As she was praying over me, telling these things to leave my body in the name of Jesus, this unbelievable peace washed over me from my head to my toes. It was a very tangible real feeling. The sickness I felt left along with it. My mind was at peace, and my body was at peace. I got up, took a bucket shower and joined the group on the trip to the village. In the meantime, we were 3 hours late leaving that morning because of car trouble. Even that small detail was orchestrated by God, allowing me time to heal before the team left.

When Ashlyn was teaching me how to pray against spiritual warfare, she said that these demons will try to get back in my head.

She told me not to leave my mind open even a crack or they will come back in. Sure enough, that night they reentered through visions and sickness. If I closed my eyes, I would get snippets of visions that were disturbing. I stayed awake all night so I wouldn't see those visions. The next morning, I told Ashlyn what happened, and she prayed over me, casting them out and speaking the powerful name of Jesus. I knew from that point on I had to recognize this immediately when it happens and speak the name of Jesus myself.

The next few days I seemed to be feeling better. I felt those evil spirits come upon me and immediately rebuked them, out loud, using Jesus' name. I could tell a huge difference in my mindset, feeling peace instead of torment. I was able to experience, with the team; many healings take place, and see God work through our team to minister to people of Sierra Leone.

In Acts 8:5-8 it says, "Philip went to people of Samaria and told the people there about Christ. Crowds listened intently to what he had to say BECAUSE OF THE MIRACLES HE DID. Many evil spirits were cast out, screaming as they left their victims, and many who were lame were healed, so there was much joy in that city!"

#123…Racquetball Court

I play racquetball. A few years ago, I lived in an apartment complex that had a court that I used a lot! One day while I was practicing, I sensed a spirit of fear inside the court. It was eerie! There had been a murder recently in one of the apartments and it seemed that fear was sweeping through the complex. I said out loud, "In the name of Jesus Christ, fear, leave!" Immediately I sensed that it was gone! Sometimes it can be that simple!

I think my command sent the spirit away from the whole complex as fear was no longer noticed.

#124…Black Birds

When Carla came for deliverance at our house, we told all evil spirits that they were not allowed in our home! She shared about how spirits followed her all around, all the time, which included touching her in many places. She commented that, while in our home, they were not around her.

We never see more than a bird or two in our yard and they are usually cardinals, robins or some such thing. But, when we looked in front of our house, there were about 50 large black birds (don't know what breed) in our yard! It seems there was an angelic "force field" keeping the evil spirits out and they were attracting the black birds!

#125…Depression Go!

"I don't know what's wrong with me!" Susan said to us, "I feel so anxious and depressed!" This was right after church too and we were still in the sanctuary! We've known her for 13 years, since she was 10, and she frequently comes to us asking for wisdom that young women sometimes need.

Quietly, near her ear, I said, "In the name of Jesus, depression, go!" The spirit of depression that was sitting on her, went!

#126…Like Birds

My name is Bob Hammond.

I was at my usual prayer spot, a quiet pond, when the Lord showed me that on our annual mission trip to Oaxaca, Mexico, I would be attacked by demons like a flock of birds. This didn't surprise me since we normally saw manifestations of Satan prior to our departure in order to distract us. So, a few demons coming at me, I thought, were no big deal. I should have realized that if the Lord was showing me something, I should pay attention especially since I was the leader of the trip!

Shortly after our arrival, I began to have unholy sexual thoughts about two of the women there. I knew them, their kids and husbands, so why was I thinking this way?! I never had before. They weren't just fleeting thoughts that I could put out of my mind, you know, like 2 Corinthians 10:5 says. No, these were tormenting thoughts that would not go away! If their husbands knew what I was thinking, they would have punched me in the mouth!

I didn't know what to do so I just suffered through it. After returning home, and through subsequent trips, this never happened again.

We had more salvations and healings on that trip than any other. When I thought about this, then it dawned on me; this is what the Lord had meant by demons swarming on me, and I had completely forgotten about it! Had I cast them off of me by saying, "In the name of Jesus Christ, spirits causing me to think this way, go!" then they would have left. Live and learn!

Hey, in spite of it all, the trip was a success and God got the glory!

#127…Lesbian Spirit

Emily called us on a Saturday morning. I didn't know her but my wife did, but only in a casual way. She was a very prominent leader and highly respected member of one of the largest churches in town. She called us because she knew we believed in casting demons out of people and thought maybe her very surprising torment was from demons. She said, "I don't know what to do. For several days I've been obsessing over having sex with women. Can you help me?" We told her to come on over. She was embarrassed so she didn't tell her husband about it, but came over to our house that afternoon.

We did what we normally do: probed her for information. She had never had sex with women and had never wanted to or even thought of it. She had a "very good sex life" with her husband and had not done anything that could have brought a lesbian spirit to her. But, there was one thing; her teenage daughter had come home from school saying, "I think I might be bi-sexual." Her daughter had been taught by someone the lie that any kind of sex with any gender is OK and so on and so on. We determined that the lesbian spirit that had gotten on her daughter, had jumped on to her: not in her, but on her.

She forgave her daughter for believing the lie and confessed her sin of not confronting the lie head-on. We then commanded the demon to leave in the name of Jesus Christ.

She never had another thought about sex with women! The lesbian spirit had left her. Praise the Lord!

#128…Fear

Alejandra had come to the USA from Guatemala. A lot of bad things go on there and fear is a common challenge for those people. When she started coming to our Bible study, she always seemed to be on edge and afraid…she was even afraid of our sweet, little, fluffy dog, Puffy. Puffy never did anything that would remotely indicate that anyone should be afraid of her! She would just roll onto her back and say, in dog language, "Love me!" But Alejandra would not get anywhere near Puffy!

She was afraid of Puffy, fearful of walking around on her college campus (Someone is following me!) and afraid of being in her bedroom alone! We determined that there was a spirit of fear *on* her, not *in* her. We commanded it to leave her in the name of Jesus Christ and she immediately noticed that it was no longer there. Before we ministered to her, she could tell it was right behind her. A spirit of fear left her and did not come back.

Oh yes, I must mention that she and Puffy are now best friends and Puffy sits on her lap during Bible study!

#129…Mind Fog

It was time for finals and one of my Christian students, Grace, came to me and asked for prayer. She said she was unable to think clearly. She had some sort of "mind fog." I said, "Do you think it is an evil spirit?" She said, "Yes!" Coming from Africa, she had no delusions about whether evil spirits exist because dealing with them is a common occurrence there!

I commanded any mind fog spirits to come off of her in the name of Jesus Christ. She immediately noticed that they were gone and confirmed it to me later as well.

She did great on her finals too! God cares about our every need!

#130…Unholy Spirits Touching

My name is Rajendran from Rameswaram.

I was affected by unholy spirits. I could not sleep at night. When I tried to sleep, I could feel the demons touching my legs and hands and then talk in my ears. Then it would grab my male reproductive organ. Therefore, I suffered a lot.

Then I came to this meeting and I slept well, no problem! God delivered me from these unholy spirits.

Chapter 11
Individuals Under 20 Years Old

This is a separate category because we see interesting things with people under 20. First, we see, like in the Bible, that parents have a big impact on deliverance of their children. There's the Gentile woman's daughter, (Matthew 15:21-28 & Mark 7:24-30), and the man's son (Matthew 17:14-21, Mark 9:14-29 & Luke 9:37-42). Numerous times we've done deliverance with teenagers and the parents, who aren't sure if they really believe in deliverance, have more authority over the demons than we do. We like to have family members involved for this reason.

Second, it seems that with older teens we are able to expel the spirits quite easily. They haven't had time to root in and secretly become part of the person, so to speak. They know something is wrong and don't like it while older individuals tend to think, "This is just how I am."

Younger children and pre-teens present some challenges. First, they aren't really sure what is going on and have a tendency to go along with whatever they are told. If they think coughing is supposed to happen, they may cough on purpose. In addition, they may not really want to be there but are because mom and dad want them to be there.

I recently was ministering to a young teen and the demon was causing her to shake violently but wasn't coming out. I told her to take charge over the spirit herself and she said, "I don't want to." I asked, "Why not?" "I don't know" was the response. Her deliverance was limited. If mom and/or dad are there, they may not want to confess sins for fear of punishment when they get home. And finally, it is likely that whatever their problems are, they probably came from mom and dad so they may not want to fess up to their sins either.

Whatever hindrances there may be, we won't do deliverance on a child unless at least one of the parents is there. (And we have learned that the parent should have gone through deliverance themselves.) They need to be involved and see what is going on with their children.

It is an awesome thing to see a suicidal, cutting teen be set free by the Lord!

#131...I Want To Be A Boy

I was asked to preach on live TV in India. I did and it was broadcast to many nations across the globe (My wife watched it live in America.). Before I did, the praise band was awesome and the lead singer, Sarah, was 19, beautiful and sang like a bird. As I listened and worshiped during the last song before I took the stage, I didn't want it to end.

When I finished my teaching on deliverance, she spoke to me and I have to admit, I was surprised by what she had to say.

Sarah was raised in a Christian home in India, something that is quite unusual as Hinduism dominates the religious landscape. She loved the Lord, but she had issues and asked me to minister to her to cast out spirits of fear. Three of us ministered to her and did just that.

As we continued to talk with her, she told us that she hated being a girl and wanted to be a boy! She said that women are mistreated in India (Yeah, no kidding!) and women were under the thumbs of men. So, she wore clothes typical of boys and acted like boys do. She also told us that when she was little, an astrologer had told her parents that she was supposed to be born as a boy, but was mistakenly born as a girl. This was a curse that was put on her and she began to live it out. Thankfully, she had not yet lived it out sexually. We appreciated her forthrightness and she was willing to repent and have us minister to her some more.

Sarah sincerely repented of wanting to be a boy and thanked God for making her a girl. She forgave all those, especially the astrologer, who promoted the idea that she should be/act like a boy. We cast demons out of her and asked God to break the "boy" curse on her.

I stayed in touch with her and five years later, she told me she thanks God every day for making her a girl and for her femininity. Praise the Lord!

#132...Stop Hiding!

Maribel was from Mexico. She was a high school student of mine, age 18. I already knew her mom (Isabel) and brother (Pablo), a 14 year old freshman, from previous ministry with her. She called me on the phone with a panicked voice, "I almost just killed myself!" she said. "We'll be right there." was my reply and my wife and I went over to their apartment.

When we walked in, she grabbed hold of me and cried. We calmed her down and called her mom. We agreed to come over another day to minister deliverance, when her mom would be home, and told her to call us if she needed anything in the meantime. We left after we knew she would be OK and her brother was there.

Prior to returning, I had notified many friends and deliverance team members what we would be doing and to please pray for us and call me if they sensed something we needed to know. When we arrived to the home a few days later, we interviewed them to find all possible entry points of demons, forgave those people involved and she confessed her own sins and repented. Then we began to command evil spirits out in the name of Jesus Christ. Demons would start to manifest and then back off. We were stuck and not progressing like we should. We asked the Lord what to do. About that time my cell phone rang. It was one of the ones praying for us. He said, "All I see is a stairway." I was looking at the stairway in their home at that very moment. I knew what it meant. I said, "Let's go upstairs." And up we went into Maribel's bedroom.

Once there, we continued the ministry and the spirits quickly began to manifest. As we commanded them out, she started screaming and throwing pillows off her bed (many!). Pablo ran out of the room crying and my wife went after him to calm him down. As I commanded demons out, I told Isabel to join me knowing that, being her mom, she had more authority over the spirits than we did. "Salganse en el nombre de Jesus! Vayanse!" ("Leave in the name of Jesus! Go away!") We both said this and I sometimes spoke in English.

Before long and after all the pillows had been dispersed around the room, the screaming stopped and Maribel lay quietly on the bed. I recognized this as a rouse by the demons so I said, "Stop hiding! Come out!" They quickly responded with more screaming only this time we knew we were close to the end.

When she quieted down, I put my hand gently on her shoulder as she lay on the bed and said in Spanish, so her mom would understand, "Como te sientes senorita?" ("How do you feel young lady?") "I feel empty." she said in English. Empty is good! We hear that a lot and it indicates that the spirits are gone. We prayed, thanked and glorified God who had delivered this sweet young soul!

We encouraged her to fill the "emptiness" with the Word of God.

Why did we need to go upstairs? I don't know, but the Lord does and it made all the difference! Praise the Lord!

#133...Thank You Jesus!

Faith was the girl next door: the one every mom wants her son to date. She was a great believer, lived righteously and exhibited the fruit of the spirit. She loved the Lord and wanted to please Him.

Then she went to college.

Florida State was a party school, as most large universities are, and she quickly joined the party scene with her new found "freedom." She lost her virginity that she had previously guarded (booze will do that to you) and since she couldn't undo what she had done, she reasoned, "I might as well enjoy sex now." She gave herself to many boys.

As time went on, she became more and more depressed. She even got to the point where she couldn't eat. If she tried, she would throw up against her will. She was losing weight, couldn't sleep and was at her wits end.

Her cousin had been through deliverance a few years earlier and she had noticed a great, positive change in her, so she contacted us, drove to Kentucky and participated in deliverance.

She was sincere and truly repentant as she confessed her sins, forgave all involved in her downfall and turned back to the Lord. We were all very proud of her! Of course, when you cooperate fully, the evil spirits have no legs to stand on and have to go. They did! Her depression left, she ate and her weight came back and she was back on track with God! Then her mouth wouldn't stop telling her friends, that she knew had demons, that they needed deliverance too.

When we finished deliverance with Faith, she got on her knees, raised her hands high on the air, and with tears streaming down her face, she said, "Thank you Jesus!"

#134...Mirror, Mirror On The Wall

We had cast demons out of Cassie before. She was one of my students in high school and was 17 years old. Part of her issue had been a mirror in her room that she had gotten in a second-hand store. She would see a woman in a white dress in the mirror and it scared her! After the deliverance, we told her to get rid of the mirror and she and her mom agreed.

Several months later, she told me at school that she was having terrible nightmares every night. My wife and I went to her home to minister to her. Then I asked, "What did you do with the mirror?" "My mom put it in the closet." "Where is it now?" "Behind my bed." I wanted to pull my hair out! It is easy to assume that people will do the sensible thing and remove something that definitely has evil spirits attached to it! But, people just don't always realize spiritual realities and that "get rid of it." means "Throw it away."

I looked behind the bed, right next to where her head would be, and there it was. I got permission from her mom to personally throw it in the dumpster outside and that's what I did and made sure it broke into pieces.

The nightmares stopped permanently!

#135…Hindu God Poster

When we entered Chaha's apartment, the first thing we saw was a poster on the wall of the most common Hindu gods. I had seen this many times before in India, but never in America, and there were about 20 gods on it.

Chaha was one of my 17 year old high school students who was from Nepal originally. She knew I believed in prayer, specifically Christian prayer, and asked me one day in school if I would pray for her mom who was having terrible back pain. I said yes and added that I usually go pray for people in person. So, she asked her mom that night and then told me in school that my wife and I could come over to pray for her.

Before praying for her mom, I asked about the poster and if they had spirits in the house. She said the lights go on and off sometimes for no reason and the refrigerator door opens and closes by itself as well. They also said they sensed a presence at times. They gave us permission to cast the spirits out and so we went into every room and commanded them out in the name of Jesus Christ. We could sense a definite presence in the kitchen too until after we had cast them out. I said, "If you want the spirits to leave and not come back, you need to get rid of that poster because it attracts them." They agreed, especially Chaha's younger brother, who was tired of all the goings on in the house! He was a Christian and was going to church regularly along with their older sister, but Chaha and her parents were still Hindu.

I told her parents that we needed to tell them about Jesus before we could continue, so for about an hour we preached Jesus Christ from Genesis on! They all said, "Jesus is Lord." and believed that God raised Him from the dead.

We then ministered to Chaha's mom and commanded the spirit of infirmity out of her. She coughed the demons out and with our backs turned to her, Chaha coughed them out too! So I continued to minister to mom and my wife to Chaha!

Back at school, I asked her how her mom was and how things were going in the home. Her mom was healed, there were no more spirit manifestations and they removed the Hindu poster. I asked what they did with it and she said, "They [her parents] put it in their bedroom." What?! Do they want spirits in their bedroom?! The next day she said they took it out of their bedroom and when I asked what they did with it, her reply was, "My mom gave it to her sister." What?! Does she want her sister to have the spirits in her house?! Finally, I was told they got rid of it altogether!

#136…Nightmares

Sarita was one of my high school students here in Bowling Green, KY. She was 16 and originally from Mexico. She was being tormented and was having nightmares so that she could not sleep. Truancy was becoming a problem because of it. She also complained that she and her family were seeing "shadows moving" in their home. Her mom invited us to come over in order to expel the spirits. My wife and I agreed.

When we entered, we were on the lookout for images related to Roman Catholicism since we knew they were from such a background (Roman Catholicism, especially in Latin America, is a perversion of Christianity.). To our surprise, we didn't see anything that struck us. So, we prayed and commanded all spirits out in Jesus' name.

Then I had the thought to go into Sarita's bedroom. I didn't want to ask, because, what 16 year old wants one of her teachers going into her bedroom even with mom there! I obeyed the Lord, asked, and they enthusiastically agreed, so the four of us went in. We started commanding spirits out of the room in Jesus' name and to our surprise, Sarita started coughing out demons! So, we changed our focus to her and continued casting them out of her.

The next day in school, she said she felt so much better and slept "like a baby."

Later, she said they never saw another shadow in her home. We felt like, since her home was in a trailer park known for illegal drug activity, spirits were roaming around the park at their own will and were sort of "passing through" when they came to her home. Well, they weren't allowed in there anymore! A-men!

#137...Teenage Torments

I have a daughter and son. We spent this last weekend going through deliverance. It was so powerful. There were years worth of bondages broken for me and my family this day. There were many struggles between the three of us. There were sexual demons, addictions, anger, and generational curses/demons that were broken and delivered that day.

My daughter, prior to having this done, was so miserable, depressed, and was so pale and frail. After this deliverance she now has color back to her face, she is smiling, she is happy, she is not angry anymore. She states she feels so light now. She said her face was so heavy before and she felt she could not smile. Now she can't stop smiling.

My son stated he felt lighter. His smile returned and he states he doesn't feel so angry anymore and he doesn't obsess over sexual thoughts and feelings anymore. He stated he felt a chain actually being broken.

I have felt more peaceful. I am not tormented anymore. I literally felt a weight being lifted off me. It is powerful the difference that I feel inside. I no longer feel like I am being torn in half between good and evil.

During this deliverance, one of the gentlemen that was involved, asked about a cabin. Later my husband had a vision of this cabin. When we arrived home Saturday, I asked my husband to draw it for me. He knew every detail down to the roof, the driveway and the windows. It was amazing. God had revealed to my husband the very spot where it all started for me. That was the place I first drank, did drugs and where I lost my virginity. That is the place where the demons really took root inside me. I found out later that the man who mentioned the cabin, said his daughter had been having nightmares about this cabin including dark figures in the cabin.

If I could tell everyone I would about this. I can't begin to explain the amazing after effects. To have God take away this bondage to no longer be chained and bound. You literally pack around a weight to do things that you don't want to do but have to. It's like you are there and can see and know what's going on but you have no say. You can't control yourself, but you deal with the aftermath, depression, guilt, anxiety, and the fear. And then it is all just lifted and taken away. I stand in AWE of the mighty God we serve.

Four years later, all the words in this testimonial are still true.

#138...Longing For Love

My name is Jeevanesan from Karaikudi.

I was in a Hindu family. We got saved as a family. I am 20 years old now and am doing my college studies.

I had no peace in me and I was longing for love. Because I had an anger problem, I lost my parents' love and I hated myself a lot. But, in this seminar, God has done great things to me and I don't have words to express my gratitude to the Lord and the team who came from the USA to conduct this seminar.

Some days before while I was playing cricket, I got a pain in my shoulder and it was troubling me a lot. I applied ointment to it but the pain didn't leave me. But now, while the time of ministry was going on in my group, the team prayed and commanded the spirit of pain to leave me, immediately I got healed and delivered of the spirit! I am very happy now!

#139...Nobody Liked Me

My name is Rajesh from Trichy.

I am 19 years old and I came with a Gypsy group. I was born and brought up in a Hindu family and my family is very poor. My family was rejected by everyone and I was addicted to every bad habit possible. There was not even 1% good in me. I was a rowdy [He means that he was a violent, evil person that usually runs with a gang in India] young man in my area doing all kinds of nonsense. Even the police would not approach me and when they heard my name they would just go away. I was in such a state. Nobody liked me. Nobody wanted to be with me. Besides that, my mother and father were also drunkards.

A church nearby our village did evangelism and one day I was touched by their evangelism. I was seeking after peace and could not find it. Finally, I received the God kind of peace through their prayers. I went to their church, but there was no change in my behavior or activities. So my pastor sent me to this seminar.

Here in this class, for the first two days, I could not control myself. I and the other gypsy boys kept talking and walking in and out. But, Daddy and the Transformation team showed unconditional love and we were attracted to their godly love.

I had no fear to do any kind of evil thing, but I had fear to stand before a microphone and speak a few words. This is the first time in my life that I have stood before a microphone and shared my testimony. I got delivered from a spirit of fear. For me, this is a great deliverance.

I had lustful thoughts about many girls. When I got delivered, the spirit of lust came out through my eyes and hands. I also got delivered from spirits of rejection, unforgiveness, anger, intimidation and many other spirits.

During the class, I got water baptized and renamed Elijah. It was a joyful moment in my life. I have decided to live a godly life.

The group training was a blessing to me. During this training, I got to cast many demons out of other people and I can now boldly say that I can cast out any kind and any number of demons.

It is God who strengthens me. Now I am so happy. I thank God for giving me this wonderful opportunity. I also thank daddy and Transformation team for caring for us and loving us. Thank you.

#140…Charlie Charlie

Around 2015, there was an occult "game" going around schools called "Charlie Charlie." Students would put a pencil on a desk and say, "Oh Charlie Charlie, move this pencil!" Kids thought it was harmless; but sometimes, the pencil moved! Little did they realize, they were inviting evil spirits into their lives.

Betsy called us crying one afternoon, "I don't know what's wrong with me! I'm so anxious!" She was 16 at the time and her mom, who we knew well, drove her to our home. She arrived shaking and very anxious and crying. We asked her to tell us exactly when she started to feel this way and it was when she was watching other kids play Charlie Charlie in school earlier that day. She was just *watching* it! It just goes to show you how sly demons can be and how vigilant we should be when we are near any kind of occult activity!

We had her confess her sin of watching the "game" and she forgave those who were playing it. Then we commanded the spirits out in Jesus' name. She coughed out two demons! The spirits were gone and did not return! Praise the Lord!

#141...Unseen Stalker

A deliverance occurred in 2003 while I was in a mountain city named Kodiakanal in India. I was up there basically to visit some friends and cool off from the heat down on the plains. A lady who had been to one of our Transformation classes there in Kodiakanal brought a young college age girl to see me while I was visiting at a church there.

It was one of the quickest deliverances I have ever been a part of. The young lady felt that she was being stalked by a college professor and was fearful for her life. She informed me that wherever she went, she would experience some kind of manifestation of this professor's presence that would make her think that he always knew where she was. I asked her if she had ever experienced anything like this before. She looked at me somewhat astonished, and asked me how I knew that. I told her that I just had an idea that it might be true. Within 20 to 25 minutes we worked our way to the root of the problem. When she had been a very small school girl, she was walking to school one day along the street. There was an old man that she walked by that was using a machete. He turned around and chased her, yelling at her, telling her she should be in school. It scared her half to death. It was at that time that a spirit of fear entered into her and tormented her at different periods of time in her life with the thought that someone was following her to do her harm.

The deliverance was fairly simple. I spoke to her about forgiving the old man with the machete and she was willing. So I led her in a prayer where she forgave the man and then I asked her to breathe out and I commanded the evil spirit of fear to leave her. She was delivered within a few minutes.

#142...Epileptic

We were about to enter the church sanctuary when a girl, maybe 12 years old, collapsed with an epileptic seizure. People started scrambling around, looking for medical professionals. I asked her mom, "Can I pray for her?" She responded with a nod so I knelt down and said, "In the name of Jesus Christ, come out!" She coughed and out it came. She got up and went in to church! (In Mark 9:17-27, Matthew 17:14-18 and Luke 9:37-43 it is recorded that Jesus healed the boy with epilepsy by driving out an evil spirit).

#143…Cutting

This is a deliverance story which taught me a lot of lessons.

We met with a middle school girl who had had suicidal thoughts and had been a 'cutter' for years. It was so bad the school escorted her to her classes so she had no opportunity to find 'things to cut with' in route to school (She had been known to take pencil sharpeners apart to use the blade.). She was on medications for her depression, and had been hospitalized many times, none of which seemed to help. She and her family came to us for deliverance. We spent a weekend deliverance session with her and her mother was also present (as we do not minister to minors without a parent present). As my husband said "her arms looked like a meat grinder had gotten hold of them."

The young lady did MUCH better for a few months but then resumed cutting. We later learned that she had a very poor relationship with her mother who was extremely controlling. We believe that she resumed cutting as a coping mechanism and perhaps subconscious pay-back to her mom for how she treated her. After this experience, we determined that we would no longer do deliverance on a minor without his/her parents having gone through deliverance prior in order to eradicate spirits which are contributing to the child's behaviors.

LESSON LEARNED…we have not had occasion to see this family again to determine how it turned out.

#144…Parent-Teacher-Student Conference

"Will you pray for me?" was Sahila's request before school started, "I am feeling depressed." It was the second to last day of school in 2013 and Sahila, age 17, asked me for prayer. I hadn't noticed, since she wore loose clothes, that she had lost a lot of weight. When I prayed for her, she began to manifest an evil spirit so I said, "I think we need to do this after school and with your mom's approval." She agreed and asked her mom that night. The next day, the last day of school, Gloria, her mom, picked her up from school and took her to our home for ministry.

When we asked her for her story, she told us that they were from Guatemala (Sahila spoke English but Gloria didn't.) and when they lived there, her dad had an affair with a witch. Sahila found out about it and told her mom so the witch did witchcraft, actually sent a curse against Sahila. There had been ongoing problems with her ever since that happened as a result of the curse, and it became so bad she had become unable to eat. When she tried to eat, she would throw up. It was not on purpose...she wanted to eat but couldn't. This is why she was losing so much weight.

After we had her forgive her dad and the witch, we cut ungodly soul ties and began to command the spirits out. She proceeded to cough out demons forcefully and felt much relief. She told us she could feel the demon come up out of her stomach and scrape her lip as it was coming out. This was new for us! Apparently, it was jabbing her like a knife on the inside causing her food to come up.

As we continued to command spirits out, her head began to shake back and forth violently and her hair, always in perfect form, was going everywhere. Screaming came with it...loud screaming! Her mom backed off the couch and my wife and I got closer until the demons were gone and she was at peace.

As they were leaving to go home, Gloria got out her wallet and asked me how much money I wanted. I simply said, "Just give God glory and thank him. We don't want anything."

After that, blood started seeping out the pores on her face. This was an indication that the blood curse put on Sahila by the witch had been broken.

So that was how the ordinary, everyday parent teacher conference went!! As you might expect, Sahila's eating went back to normal and she gained the needed weight back! Praise the Lord!

#145...Hurt Child

I felt a lot of release on the last day that really needed to come out. I experienced healing from the hurt child in me that had come from the lack of feeling love from my father.

Thank you Jesus!
And thank you for the deliverance team!

For more stories of individuals under 20 years old see #'s 49. 81.

Chapter 12
Haunted Homes

This is another category that people want to know about. This is probably for two reasons: they see a lot of shows on TV about it or they, or someone close to them, have experienced it. Whatever the case, it is very real and the "ghosts" are evil spirits (In the Bible, "ghost" and "spirit" is the same word in Greek, *pneuma*.).

Even the disciples were freaked out when they saw Jesus walking on the sea thinking it was a phantom (Matthew 14:26, Mark 6:49, John 6:19).

So, why are they there in the first place? There are a number of reasons. First, there are artifacts in the home that attract them. Anything connected to a false god will likely have spirits attached to it. A seemingly harmless souvenir may provide a ride to America when the person returns.

Second, the person is living a sinful lifestyle and demons are following him/her around and settling into their home as well. They are sometimes in the person and sometimes nearby.

Third, there was a tragic death in the home. Yes, murder, for example. The spirit is not the spirit of the dead person, but a spirit familiar with him/her. It may impersonate the person or give other signs that it has a connection to him/her.

Fourth, witchcraft or occult practices were conducted there and the spirits that were brought in, stay.

Fifth, there are spirits in the area. A trailer park where illegal drug activity is known to occur is a good example. Spirits are roaming around the area and pass through the home on a regular basis.

Sixth, the reason is unknown. We just don't know, but cast them out anyway!

How does one get rid of them? Whenever we go into a home infested with spirits, we try to cover all the bases; we have the person confess and repent of any sins they did there that would attract them, we have the person forgive anyone else that lived in the home previously that did sinful stuff, we look for anything that could attract them (like skeletons, suspect artifacts, Roman Catholic images, weird mirrors, etc.) and remove them and we go from room to room and command spirits out in the name of Jesus Christ. We especially include the resident in actively commanding spirits out since they live there and have more authority over the place than we do.

When commanding spirits out, there are basically two approaches; one works and one doesn't. There's the nice, polite, "I'm afraid of them and don't want to make them mad at me" approach that doesn't work, "Please Mr. Evil Spirit, leave my home in the name of Jesus. You aren't welcome here so, if you don't mind, head on out the door and go away. There's an empty home over there across the street and we promise not to bother you." And then there's the authoritative, Luke 10:19 approach, "All spirits in this house, scram!! I'm not asking you, I'm ordering you!! How dare you come in here and invade our privacy!! *Get out now in the name of Jesus Christ!!*" They hear that approach!

We have never failed in getting rid of the ghosts. There have been times when the spirits are persistent and don't want to leave. But, the resident becomes more persistent and keeps after them until they are gone!

#146…Al B. Sure!'s Home

It was the fall of 1988 and R & B singer Al B. Sure! (Stage name) had just come out with his smash hit *Nite and Day*. His parents were close friends of mine from church and lived in Goshen, NY.

Knowing that I believed in evil spirits, they told me they had an "issue." It seems that frequently when they returned home, they would see a woman in their front window but when they went inside, she was gone. It was always the same woman too. In addition, they would sometimes hear inexplicable noises coming from that room. They felt it must be a ghost. They asked me to come over and try to send it away and I agreed to come as long as they agreed to follow through on what I recommended.

When I arrived, I looked through the house to see if there was anything that looked like it might attract evil spirits. There were a couple of "iffy" things, but when I went into the front living room, the same one that the woman would appear in, there was a picture on the wall of a woman. I can't say it was "erotic," but I can say that it was somewhat sensuous. The strangest thing was that when you walked through the room, her eyes seemed to follow you all the way! Yikes!

I said, "That is weird! I'd get rid of it!" They did, we prayed for all spirits to leave and they never saw the "woman" or heard noises again!

#147...Scary Face

One night I had to go to a business meeting at my church and left my 6 year old daughter at home with her 16 year old brother. I had no longer gotten into the meeting when I got a very disturbing phone call from my son who told me I had to get home NOW! I rushed home to find my daughter terrified and crying...she told me that she had seen a scary person in her room right after her brother had tucked her into bed. She said he was *very* scary and mean, and his face was like her dad's. Her father had recently divorced me, and we had suffered many years of verbal and emotional abuse from him. I prayed with her and in the name of Jesus we cast out any powers from the enemy which were in our home and prayed protection over each one of us.

We lived in the home for a couple of years after that episode and we never had another scary, mean person in our home. We are confident that there was a demon in our home and that God delivered us from the fear and demon from that time on until the present...20 years later.

#148...Haunted Home

We were contacted by a prominent successful businessman in the Nashville area. He had been having spirits attacking him daily in his 'beautiful mansion' of a home for a very long period of time. He was tormented when he tried to sleep at night. He had spirits touching him as he tried to sleep. He had tried having pastors come anoint with oil and pray but the spirits continued to torment him.

When we arrived, we tried to identify possible things which could be attracting the spirits. We were unable to identify anything which seemed to be the attraction. However, in the name of Jesus we commanded the spirits to leave. The spirits were less frequent but did not leave and continued to torment him.

Often, spirits come into homes because the individual has some sin that needs to be dealt with which has attracted them. Based upon that prior knowledge, we decided to meet with the man, have him confess sins, forgive people who needed to be forgiven and cut ungodly soul ties between the offenders. We then commanded any spirits in or on him to leave in the name of Jesus.

The spirits' presence diminished and it was improving. However, he did not have total freedom. At that time we told him to TAKE AUTHORITY and command the demons to leave because they did not have authority over him and in the name of Jesus they had to go…after doing this for a couple of weeks the spirits left and have not returned.

At times the individual himself has to **take authority** in the name of Jesus to get full deliverance.

#149…Court Is In Session

I did see a satanic court being conducted on the platform of a new Nazarene church (along with 7-8 other kids) when I was 5. The church was going to be dedicated the next Sunday, and Satan (or one of his main guys) was on a throne and he was surrounded by a whole court of attendants. All of the kids got tired of the prayer meeting going on in the old building (just a basement really, that never had a building put on top of it), and we went around into the lobby of the new building, looked through the glass doors leading into the sanctuary, and there he was… spooky music playing, and all the figures illuminated from the inside out, almost like hologram light figures at the ghost house in Disney, except that this was 10 years before Walt even imagined Disney World… and also well before holograms and the laser were even invented.

It was pretty scary stuff.

Several times they disappeared and came into our midst invisibly, and we were ice cold from the inside out when this would happen. We were too scared to move during these times; only my friend Daniel managed to croak, "He is in us now!" Then the scene would light up again on the platform and we would feel normal.

That might make a pig run off a cliff. It sure did make us run out of the new church building!

It was in 1958 or 1959. I think it was in the fall.

My rational mind was functioning because I remember looking across the street. There was a Tasty Freeze with a sign of blinking yellow lights, and I was thinking, "Could this be an optical illusion caused by reflections from that sign?" And figuring out that this could not be the case.

Afterward, we went around the outside of the building and peeked through the windows leading into the Sunday school classrooms in the basement. In each one on, the little table in the front of the classroom, there was a little animated figurine of the figure on the throne in the sanctuary, also illuminated from within.

We told the adults about it but they just thought we were telling ghost stories and had imagined the whole thing.

Years later, when I was in an art collection at my dad's library, I randomly opened a book of ancient woodcuts of oriental deities or royals (resting my eyes from a go at the math book) and the person we had seen on the throne was depicted and I then realized that others had seen him too.

#150...Skull Island

We didn't know what to expect when we entered. We were told they were seeing spirits in the home and wanted to be rid of them. We pointed out things that we thought could attract them and then left it up to the people to either believe us and do what we recommended or not.

When we first entered, I noticed a mirror on the front door that looked like a Sun god to me. They said they sometimes see a woman in it. Gee, ya think they should get rid of it?!

The predominant things we saw were skulls. We would enter a room, not every room, and say, "Yes, there are spirits here." Invariably we would find skulls somewhere in the room. One room, a bedroom, had spirits but we couldn't see any skulls. I said, "What's in the closet?" It was locked. They unlocked it and, you guessed it, there were clothes with skulls on them.

In a couple of rooms we didn't sense anything and they would agree that they never had anything weird happen in these rooms. No skulls there!

We did the normal thing and commanded all spirits to leave in the name of Jesus Christ and told the residents that if they wanted the spirits out, they needed to get rid of the mirror and all the skulls too.

Did they do it? We don't know, but we never heard any more complaints from them either.

#151...Evil Twins

We had recently moved into a small rental house in the country in Ohio. One day my wife, Sue, said to me that, during the time we had lived there, our two small children didn't sleep well at night, and whenever she would go into the small bedroom that the children shared she felt something strange. She asked me if I would go into their room and try to discern if there was something spiritual there. Upon entering the little bedroom, I saw, in the Spirit, two little beings. They stood approximately two and one-half feet high and were covered completely with long hair. I sensed that they were demons with little power. I told them to leave in the name of Jesus and not to return.

From that day, our children slept well in the little room and Sue felt nothing more unusual. Our children were too small to be aware of any of this and everything happened without their knowledge.

#152...Depression

We were called to a home that had strange things happening in it. There were noises, depression, shadows that were seen and other things. We went from room to room and looked for things that might attract spirits like items attached to a false god or just plain weird stuff. Then we prayed for all spirits to leave each room.

When we entered the parents' room, I felt depression and my wife said "Look, I'm crying!" We later learned, "Mom" would always lie on her bed severely depressed for days in this room. We cast spirits of depression out of the room.

Later, we ministered to "Mom" and cast spirits out of her too!

Immediately there was no evidence of spirits in the home and months later, no spirits were in their home, and the depression was no longer in Mom's room. Praise God!

#153...Calling On Jesus

It was 1998, almost a year after my divorce. My children and I lived in a two bedroom apartment and I was experiencing life as a single mother of three. During this time, I had gotten back into the church and was really trying to turn my life around. It was hard living and sleeping alone since my divorce, so I regularly took my youngest son out of his crib and laid him beside me. Usually, because of his erratic sleeping habits, he would end up on the pillow lying above my head.

One particular night I experienced something very unusual and scary. As I usually did, I went to my son's room and retrieved my baby from his crib, laid him by my side and turned out the lights for bed. As I attempted to fall asleep, I felt something cover my mouth. I opened my eyes and nothing was there, but my mouth was still covered and was muffled as if someone was trying to quiet me. I could not move or sit up and the first thing I thought to do was call on the name of Jesus. I began to call Jesus' name over and over again while my mouth was still covered. All you could hear was a muffled wailing of "Jesus, **Jesus**, *Jesus*." As I continued to call on the name of Jesus, I could hear my voice becoming clearer and clearer through the muffle caused by whatever it was trying to cover my mouth. It slowly and hesitantly removed its hand from my mouth.

Afterwards, I felt release and immediately jumped out of the bed, turned on the light and checked on my baby first and my sons in the other room. I then fell to my knees, prayed and thanked God for deliverance.

#154…Apartment Cleaning

June asked us to come and "pray out" the spirits that were in her family's apartment. There would be noises and dark shadows that would move around at times. We went from room to room and commanded all spirits to leave in the name of Jesus Christ. One room, in particular, seemed to have a negative presence. She confirmed that most of the things that happened happened in there.

We looked for anything that could be attracting them, but saw nothing. They believed that the previous renters had done some sort of occult related thing there such as witchcraft, so we forgave the previous renters for anything they had done.

We didn't hear or see anything while we were there, but later, and again much later, June told us that all demonic activities had ceased! "Cleaning out" an apartment can be just that simple in Jesus' name!

#155…Imaginary Friend

One of my first dealings with demons happened 24 years ago. My daughter was two years old at the time, and due to the divorce of her daddy and me, she had an imaginary friend, Floppy. Everyone thought it was cute that she had an imaginary friend. She'd talk to him in her playroom and she made me give him food and instructed me which chair he was in and many other little things. Harmless, I thought. One day while we were riding in the car, she cracked up laughing in the back

seat. I asked, "What's so funny?" Her reply, "Floppy's telling jokes!"
Around that time, I'd joined a Bible study. One day I shared about the imaginary friend. Afterward, an older lady told me she would not let a demon play with her child. I considered what she said. Then one day I commanded Floppy to leave, told him he wasn't allowed to be there and couldn't play with my daughter. Some time passed (I don't remember how long, it was so many years ago.). I noticed my sweet little girl playing quietly. I asked, "Do you play with Floppy anymore?" She replied, "No Mama, you made him leave." At that moment I realized Floppy wasn't a harmless thing.

#156...Greek Gods

Judy was single, in her 20's and lived with her mom whose home was infested with spirits. Judy had demons, which we cast out of her, and so did her mom who would not allow us to cast them out of her. Mom was active in occult practices, which she did in the home, and had numerous artifacts of Greek gods that she had brought back with her from a European vacation. I would have been shocked if there weren't spirits in this home!

One night, some of the people in our church went to their home for a party of some sort and spent the night. I don't remember why and I wasn't a part of it. There were three of four of them there. During the night, all of them experienced the same thing; invisible "hands" were felt around their throats in a choking manner, only the pressure was not enough to actually choke them. It seems the Lord protected them from harm.

At the time, we were learning about demons but had not experienced such a thing! Frankly, it scared the "begeebees" out of them! A simple, "Get away from me in the name of Jesus Christ!" would have probably sent them away and caused them to release their grip.

Shortly after this I moved away and never heard about the matter again.

For more stories involving haunted homes see #'s 71, 80, 134, 135,

Chapter 13
Anger Spirits

When I think of anger, I think of a question I get asked frequently, "I have such and such problem. Do you think it is a demon?" My answer is usually, "Have you confronted it with the Word of God?" I ask this because there are "soulish" problems people have and there are demon problems. Not every problem is a demon and all problems can be confronted with the Word.

We are to put away all anger toward people (Ephesians 4:31) but we are also to be angry at sin (Ephesians 4:26) like Jesus was toward the hard heartedness of the Pharisees (Mark 3:1-6).

A good indicator of an evil spirit of anger is when a person flies off the handle at the smallest things. They don't have control and can't stop it. And, surprisingly, they don't always want to be freed from it. They like to manipulate others with anger and they are afraid that if they no longer have it, they will lose control.

A spirit of anger can result in physical problems, abuse, drug abuse, rejection, depression, revenge, thinking about revenge, sadness, sabotaging relationships, legalism, unforgiveness, criticism, turning to a cult, self-cursing, verbal explosions, negative body language, road rage, violence and the silent treatment.

We see anger spirits a lot because it is connected to another common one: rejection. Anger is usually a fruit and rejection a root. One who has anger spirits usually has rejection ones too.

The person needs to be confronted with their issue and have the spirit(s) cast out!

#157...Road Rage

My name is Mike Durnen.

If anyone had asked me before deliverance, I would have told them I was normal, just like anybody else. Meaning:

I had little patience and an "Irish" temper, but then again – don't most people? I often allowed little-meaningless things to drive a wedge between my wife and me, which would eventually turn into a full-scale argument. I would also get quickly agitated at the little things people do, or don't do, while driving, such as: lack of using turn signals, holding up traffic in one lane to try to get into the next, tail-gating, etc. Again, I thought I was pretty normal and like most other people. However, when I learned about deliverance, I felt the Holy Spirit telling me I needed to go through it.

So, in preparation for it, I tried to be completely honest with myself and confessed on paper everything I could think of, and I do mean everything. I went as far back as I could remember and tried to bring it all out into the open – even those things I didn't think really mattered (spoiler alert: that's a demon talking). So, I went through deliverance with a wonderful team at my side, praying and ministering to me, and basically setting me free through the power of the Holy Spirit. The freedom I felt by the end of my deliverance was like nothing I had felt before. It was like a giant weight had been lifted off of my shoulders and I felt a calm and peace that could only come from God.

Unfortunately, deliverance isn't a one-and-done deal. Spiritual forces are constantly trying to turn you away from God. Think of it as a one-way tug of war with evil on one end and God on the other. The only problem is, Satan is pulling you and God is not – rather, God is waiting for you to pull yourself to Him.

Having gone through deliverance training, I can now recognize when those little voices inside my head are trying to get me to slip again and the more I stay in God's Word (Bible), the easier it is to recognize those thoughts for what they are – evil or good.

Since my deliverance, my compassion for others in need of deliverance has greatly increased – you know, the other "normal" people walking around that have no clue what Satan and his minions are doing to their lives on a daily basis. While my deliverance would be considered a fairly "calm" event, my experiences with deliverance for others has revealed to me just how radical demons can be and how much they can influence or alter a person's life.

Bottom line is that life is a daily battle and it doesn't matter whether you're a Christian (I am) or not, or a "good" person or not, Satan wants you and will do whatever he can to pull you away from God. If you think your life is going along pretty good and bump-free (I did), odds are you're right where Satan wants you and not living life as

God would have you live it.

#158…Renewed Mind

My name is Denise Keeter.

This weekend's deliverance event was life changing for me! I appreciate everyone's time. A special shout out to Teresa Jones, April Secore, Kim Breakfield, Tina Oates, Gary Thompson & Troy Hardin. My group members were kind, knowledgeable, wise & a safe place for me to share my life with. This was a sacrifice of love & it showed! The deliverance team, ALL of them, encouraged me for what I know God is equipping me to do in the future. This curriculum is powerful & better than I've experienced before, through my old church.

I had no demons to cast out but my team led me to areas of my life where unforgiveness & anger were hiding out. I let go of some major things like intimidation, cruelty, fear, bitterness! My team laid hands on me & prayed over my mind. That's exactly what I came to this event for: to renew my mind. I feel so free now. I definitely see me leading or supporting this type of event again in the future. It's my heart's desire to see people walk in freedom.

Before I left, Sharon & Troy prayed over me & my family. They gifted me their shofar and made me cry like a baby. I was so overwhelmed by God's goodness this weekend. I'm also grateful Bob asked me if I'd like to go through their training & lead with them if they are in the area at some other time. I hope the Lord will make that happen.

#159…Many Demons

Anger, rejection, witchcraft, sex, Hindu idol spirits: you name it, she had it! Joy had so many demons in her that we lost count. She had done just about everything including worshiping, as she would later say, all the Hindu gods. Her search for truth and happiness had led her to many ungodly places and choices. But, she finally ended up in the Transformation class.

As we began group ministry sessions, I found myself casting demons out of her. They came out one after the other. Sometimes the Lord would show me the next one, sometimes Joy would tell me the next one and sometimes the demon would give its name. (One of them identified itself in Hindi and I said, "No, you tell me in English!" So it said in a man's voice, "Blaaaaaaack Maaaagiiiiiic." (Joy had used black magic to try and get a boyfriend back.) Eventually I just said, "Who's next?" This went on session after session.

Now, Joy ministers to hundreds of people and I think she has helped cast demons out of more people than the number of demons that came out of her! Praise the Lord for setting Joy, and all those she ministers to, free!

#160…Bending Cast Iron

My name is Troy Hardin.

My deliverance story begins at eight years old. It starts here because it was the first time I cast a demonic spirit away and did not realize what I was doing. I was spending the night with my grandmother Mamie. I often did this as a child. She belonged to the Catholic Church just down the road from where she lived. She was unlike any Catholic I have seen, even today. She believed in the power of Jesus' name. She had always taught me that if I was in a bad situation, I could call on the name of Jesus, and He would come to my rescue.

I was spending the night with her, and we had gone to bed. I was sleeping in her guest room and was sound asleep when I woke up to an eerie feeling across my eight-year-old body. I woke up from a dead sleep to a figure standing at the foot of my bed. I could see the features quite well from the glow of the night light in the room. The figure looked like an older man crouched over with glowing eyes, and he was wringing his hands as if he was about to do something to me. I thought the devil was coming to take me to hell or God knows what. All I could say out of my frightened mouth was, "In the name of Jesus Christ, leave." It looked at me as if it was surprised I knew how to do that and left instantly.

That moment birthed something in me that would lead to a deliverance ministry. It wasn't until 37 years later I was introduced to deliverance ministry. Up until 2017, I thought deliverance was a Hollywood movie. I was asked to join a crew of missionaries to journey to India for three weeks to learn about healing and deliverance. I have been a student of the Bible for many years and had read where Jesus and the disciples cast out demons as they ministered on their journeys.

I guess I was under the impression that Christians couldn't have demons; boy, was I wrong. As we arrived in India, I could sense the activity of the demonic spirits all around me.

The first week there, we had the opportunity to minister to people before the class was to start the following week. Upon arrival at the meeting site, we were informed that we needed to go through the deliverance class before being on the team. I was skeptical, thinking I didn't need deliverance because I was already saved; what more did I need? As the class started, I quickly realized I had buried some emotions of anger and the sexual sin that I just knew I had conquered. I had anger toward my mother and other family members because of childhood events. I also had soul ties to girls. I had sexual relations in high school. Other demons I had to have cast out were from an early introduction to the porn industry. Pornography was the avenue I used to educate myself about sex. It had a more significant hold on me than I initially thought.

Since then, I have been back to India once, and that time, I was able to participate as a team member. I was allowed to minister deliverance to individuals and teach the participants. I was teaching witchcraft and the occult, and while I was teaching, one of the men in my group told me afterward that as I was teaching, he got furious at me and wanted to harm me but couldn't understand why. I told him it was a spirit of anger manifesting in him. Later we had a deliverance session on rage, and this same guy was sitting in one of those old-time school desks with the fold-over top. The desk is made of cast iron from top to bottom. He began to manifest the spirit of anger, and when he did, the demon gave him superhuman strength, and he folded the sides of that desk chair almost flat. Once we got the demon out, all four guys in the group tried to bend that chair back, and we couldn't budge it. I have never in my life seen a demon manifest like that. Since then, I have witnessed some very animated demonic activity.

Since India, I have had many opportunities to minister deliverance to others. It has been a blessing for me to have the chance to witness the freedom of so many people and build relationships with them.

After my salvation in 1994, my oldest brother was the first person in my family that I couldn't wait to tell. He gave me Scripture and told me to memorize it and always remember it, and I would do great things. That Scripture was Luke 10:19, "Behold, I give you the authority to trample on serpents and scorpions and over all the power of the enemy and nothing shall by any means hurt you." (NKJV) Little did I know what he was speaking to me at that moment.

Present-day, I am finding myself more involved with healing and deliverance ministry. I recently participated in a deliverance session involving a young lady who had battled schizophrenia earlier. She had told those of us on the team that she would be laying on her bed when she would have an episode, and she would see a figure that appeared to be a substantial-sized green slug. I have dealt with many different evil spirits, like serpent spirits, but never a slug. So, the team and I decided to research and discovered a photo of a vast green slug. We showed the image to the recipient, and she began to manifest the spirit. I wasn't sure how to deal with this spirit, so I told the spirit that I would pour salt on it if it didn't come out. Slugs cannot handle salt; for some reason, slugs will dissolve when they encounter salt. Then one of the team members suggested that I go and find some salt, so I did. I came back, and the recipient was manifesting, so I sprinkled some salt on her back, and the spirit became more animated. After doing this, the spirit came out a couple of times, and the recipient took charge and let her authority rise. Then the demons knew their jig was up, and they came out.

Jeremiah 33:3 says, "Call to Me, and I will answer you, and show you great and mighty things, which you do not know." This Scripture has become a very true statement in our lives and ministry. The Lord, through deliverance, has shown my wife and me so many great and mighty things. I believe it is just the beginning for us as we continue this journey. Each deliverance is different, and we gain new knowledge that generally helps with the next. There is great reward in being a part of setting the captives free. It is an honor and a blessing to minister to those the enemy has held in bondage and seeing them set free is priceless.

All glory be unto God!

#161…I Hate Everybody!

Naomi had a troubled childhood. The truth is, she remembered very little of it so the trauma she endured must have been severe. We know this because she could barely speak to us when we met her. But, she was very devoted to the Lord, prayed and studied the Word of God faithfully. She knew God was good and wanted the best for her. Still, she grew up in Haiti, a place where a lot of bad things happen.

She received deliverance from numerous people, at numerous times and in numerous places. She told us later that she got the most deliverance from us due to our love and patience with her. I don't say this to be prideful, but it is always good to know that you are "hitting the mark" when doing deliverance.
At one point I said, "I am speaking to the head demon that is in charge of all the other demons. I command you to give me your name!" Her face turned evil looking and rage showed up as the spirit screamed out of her

mouth, "***Hatred! I f****** hate everybody!***" Well now, there was no doubt what that spirit was!

You would not recognize her now. She just glows with the love of God! Jesus sets the captives free!

#162...Severe Anger Problem

My name is Arockia Arasi from Karaikudi.

When I came to this seminar, I was suffering from depression, fear of death, loneliness and was tormented by evil spirits; I had a severe anger problem.

In this seminar God gave me great deliverance and I received a great healing in my thought life. I received the heart to love others, and the fear of God has begun to increase in me. I received great truth from every lesson that was taught, and I learned how to lead others into deliverance.

I will be praying for this deliverance ministry to spread all over the world. Before I came to this seminar I never practiced tithing. Here I learned to give the tithes of money, fruits of the land and time. All of my life I commit my life to live as a witness. Since recently my husband passed away I was not able to come out of the spirit of sorrow. But God delivered me from the familiar spirit as well as the spirit of sorrow.

Please pray for my children and my relatives to come to know the Lord.

#163...Violent To Tender

My name is Rebekah Isaac from Thindivanam.

When my husband came back from this seminar, I really saw a great change in him. He is tender and loving and has become a new person.

But, prior to this, he was a very angry person for 11 years of our marriage. When he got angry, we would not know what would happen to us. He used to break televisions, mirrors, table fans, cooking vessels, etc. Many nights my children and I went to sleep without food because when he came in late at night he would throw the food on the floor. Many times I tried to commit suicide because of his character.

Because of the change in him, I have come to this seminar too.

#164...Lose Temper Easily

My name is S. Stanley from Salem.

I was born and brought up in a Christian family. Since my father was a missionary, I had known Jesus for the past 32 years. Although I attended Sunday services without fail and went to many conferences, my character was not changed. I fought with this kind of life, but I continuously failed to overcome. Even though I had a good job, I could not lead a good life and I could not satisfy my parents. Then, one of my friends told me about this Transformation meeting.

On the first day, when Larry was doing the teachings, it was so different to me. The teachings were unique. Every day the Word of God was deep to me.

I noticed a change that took place in me while I was traveling during the weekend of the class. I was traveling on a bus and there was a Hindu RSS man, who hated Christians, sitting near me. He was playing a Hindu slogan song on his cell phone very loud and it was annoying me. Before attending this meeting, my nature was to lose my temper very easily and become impatient. But, this time, during that disturbing situation, I did not get angry or upset. I could see patience working in me. This was amazing to me.

During the times of ministry into freedom from fear and anger, I received a major deliverance. I experienced my body getting stiff and then it was fully released and I experienced softness in my body. Previously, I fought with my mom and dad and left home and stayed away for 2 years. When I confessed my sins to God, I received deliverance from my anger problem.

In the group ministry training sessions, all of our team members were able to cast demons out. In India, it is commonly believed by many Christians that only big pastors can cast out demons. But, God has opened our eyes to see the truth that every believer can and must cast out demons.

Thanks for this ministry. I thank God for the great change that took place in me which had not happened for about 32 years.

In the Bible, I have read about the love ministry of Jesus, but here in this Inner Healing ministry I could see the same kind of ministry being done. Thank you very much for this truthful and faithful ministry.

#165…Demons Evicted

My name is Shawn Barnett.

If you would have told me 10 years ago that I would participate in the expulsion of demons, I would have told you that you were mistaken. Not that I didn't believe, but I doubted my power as a Christian. A lot of that doubt came from lack of education. Well, this weekend has opened my eyes to a war that is raging behind the eyes of so many. I not only evicted anger/temper from the very fabric of my soul but I gained knowledge and healing.

Years ago I had a foot crushed at work and I suffer from nerve damage. Remarkably though for the last two days I haven't experienced the nerve pain or my normal back pain. Even if you doubt, you have nothing to lose as long as you're willing to open yourself to honest reflection; freedom from the influence of theses spirits is so liberating.

I haven't felt so free since I can remember and God has given every one of us authority to cast them out of ourselves and those around us! I can't wait to greet the world again without the weight of confinement.

#166…Yelled At Everybody

Lun is Zomi (an ethnic group from war-torn Burma) and came to the USA in 6th grade. By the time we met her, she was in high school. She came to church with us and with her boyfriend, Suman, also Zomi, and both of them got saved! Praise the Lord!

One day she told us that she had an anger problem and wanted help. We asked questions to get more specifics about it and found out she yelled and cussed at her parents, boyfriend and other friends every day! We told her that we had enough to know that her issue was a demon and we asked her if she wanted us to cast it out. She did. (Don't assume people want things from the Lord unless they say they do.)

Her problem started when she arrived here. Kids picked on her and laughed at her because she didn't speak English yet. She became bitter and resentful and a spirit of anger entered her. A sixth grader doesn't realize that people can be jealous of you (Lun speaks four languages fluently!) so they try to pull you down.

We had her forgive all those who hurt her and confess her own sins in the matter. When it came time to confess her own sins, she said, "God, forgive me for cussing at everyone." We told her to be more specific about exactly what she said so she said, "God, forgive me for calling everybody mother f*****, ass ****, sh** head..." We were so proud of her! She didn't want us to think badly of her, but she followed our instructions and was specific! Apparently she was sincere because when we commanded the spirit of anger out of her in the name of Jesus, she immediately coughed it out. Within a few days we got feedback from her and her boyfriend who verified to us, with a smile, that his girlfriend was not cussing him, or anybody else, out! Praise the Lord!

Now, a few years later, she is still free!

#167...Angry Growl

My first experience with casting out demons was when I was about 20 years old and not actually trying to do this! I was leading a missions group in Portsmouth, VA, and one of the girls in our "family" had a boyfriend who came to visit her during the year. She said he had recently been saved and had some "outbursts of anger issues."

During his visit, she asked me to pray with him and minister to him in some areas of inner healing. I said, "Sure I would love to!" and naively jumped right into a ministry time with him! There were a lot of people including some neighbors we were witnessing to in our tiny apartment so I decided we would go into the only room with privacy which was the half bath! I boldly laid hands on him without asking permission from him or the Father and said, "In the name of Jesus..." and he cowered and let out a deep growl like a scared dog or wild animal! I was totally not expecting that and immediately opened the door as I could tell this demon was threatened and leaving and I being inexperienced, did not know what to do.

I proceeded to pray over him and we did not see any outbursts the rest of the time he was with us. I have to admit that hearing such an authentic growl coming from a human did rattle me a bit but this did lead me into further teaching on our authority in Jesus Christ and taking authority over these demons which plague people!

#168...Mother And Daughter

My name is Susanne Bowling.

I first heard about deliverance when a friend of mine went overseas and after three weeks came back home and talked about her experience. I was very interested and wanted to know more about it.

Later that year, Bob got permission from the church to have a class about deliverance and I signed up for it.

The class started in January and I believe about February or March I went to Bob and Karen's house. We talked a little about it and then I had my first deliverance about anger. The spirit of anger left me and at the same time the anger also came off of my daughter who was miles away. I remember it very well. It was a Thursday after Bible study.

Then, later on, we had group deliverance at Sharon's house which was very powerful and a lot of evil spirits left me.

Just recently, I was part of deliverance for a lady and was comparing myself a lot to her. I realized I still had some spirits in me, so after the weekend, I asked Karen, April and Kim to be part of deliverance for me. At first, spirits did not want to let go, but when I finally forgave and was honest about the things I was holding back, spirits came out and left me. My outer appearance completely changed to the best!

And now I am truly a new creation!

#169...I Severely Beat My Children

My name is Pushpa Rani from Kalayarkoil.

This is my first time attending this Inner Healing and Deliverance meeting. I had a lot of anxiety. Because of that, I had chest pain for so many years. I felt a very heavy weight in my heart.

I also had a severe anger problem. Although my son is 26 and my daughter 23, when I would get angry, I would beat them both severely. During this meeting, I came to realize that that was sin, so I repented.

When I went home, I asked for forgiveness from my children. In this meeting, I began to understand the real love of Jesus. God delivered me from my anger problem.

I was also suffering from a guilty conscience. I was not able to forgive people who spoke ill of me. But, now I am freed from all of those spirits. My chest pain is gone. God has healed me and I feel complete deliverance from bitterness, fear and anger. I give glory to the Lord Jesus Christ. I thank God for the deliverance.

#170...Broke Things And Beat People

My name is Josephine Sheela from Karaikal.
I had so much rejection in my life. My mother loved my sister and because of this, I felt I was rejected. I hated my mother, my sister and all

the others in my family. I tried to commit suicide thinking that by dying I would make my family cry. When I heard the teaching on rejection, I forgave all my family members and God delivered me from the spirits of rejection.

I had witchcraft spirits in me. When I confessed all my witchcraft activities, I experienced the spirits leaving through my mouth and hands.

I had anger problem in me. When I got angry, I used to break things, beat people and never talk with anyone for many days. When I learned about anger in this class, I confessed all my sins and God gave deliverance from the spirits of anger.

#171...Confessing Sins

During the first two days I was feeling sleepy and wasn't much interested in listening to the teachings. But, from the 3rd day, as I listened to the teachings, faith started to rise up in me and I began confessing my sins. When it came time to breathe out, I was a little hesitant, because it was a new experience for me. I began cooperating with the ministry team and began to throw up and a spirit of unforgiveness left me.

The first week was OK to me. Then the second week began and during the training time I was instructed to confess my sins to my team members. This was a little difficult for me. I was hesitating, but somehow I made up my mind and began.

There was not much deliverance the first week, but the second week, as I confessed my sins to the team members in my group, many evil spirits left me. There were spirits of fear, rejection, shame, guilt, unforgiveness, idol worship, lust of the eyes, bitterness and anger. These all came out of me through different manifestations. Now I know that these teachings and the method of deliverance make it much easier to cast out demons, both in my personal life and from others also.

Thank you very much for the transformation team. May God bless you.

#172...Lesser Of Two Troubles

Mohammad was one of my high school students from Somalia and was a Muslim. He was a good student and respectful of teachers. But, lurking beneath was uncontrollable anger.

He told me one day about his anger. He said every day he gets up and starts yelling at his family over the littlest things. In school he would get angry at a teacher or student and walk out of class without permission. He got in trouble for this but, as he said, "I know I will get into more trouble if I stay and show my anger in a bad way so if I leave, I get into less trouble." What a horrible way to live!

I asked him when it started and he said that when he was in Somalia, there was a young woman with an anger evil spirit. He tried to get it to come out by hitting her. Then the spirit spoke to him and told him if he did a certain thing with his fingers, it would come out. So, he did and when it came out, it went into him. Taking advice from a demon is a bad thing! (As a Christian, casting a demon out will never be accompanied by it coming into you. See Luke 10:19.).

I told him we could cast the demon out in the name of Jesus Christ, but he would not let me. He would not renounce his Muslim faith. As far as I know, it is still in him.

For more stories about anger spirits see #'s 21, 26, 33, 40, 46, 48, 50, 52, 53, 54, 63, 65, 87, 90, 91, 92, 93, 94, 95, 115, 137, 138, 139, 158, 159, 160, 194.

Chapter 14
Miscellaneous

This is a "catch all" category for any story that doesn't seem to fit into any of the others. But, don't be fooled! Some of the most dramatic and interesting deliverances are here. Read on!

#173...War Trauma

My name is Phil Stephens.
As a child, my siblings and I lived with our paternal grandparents. Our grandfather had an old steamer trunk in his bedroom containing items he brought back from World War One. Among them were items that are now called "trench art:" a canteen cup with a large eagle carved with his bayonet, his mess kit with the complete history of the combat he saw engraved on it. We would beg him to open the trunk and tell us stories about what he did and saw during his time in combat. At any time during the story he would develop an unusual look on his face and suddenly say, "That's all boys, go to bed." I never understood what had just happened until I spent my time in combat, from jungle to hilltop, trying to help a small country stay free from communism.

After picking up the body of a man who had just told me this was his last day and he could not wait to see his two boys after 12 months of missing them, I immediately understood the look on my grandfather's face. I will not describe the horrible wound that took the man's life, but it will be with me for the rest of my life. Tears fell from me the rest of that day and into the night thinking about those two sons whose last memory of their dad would be their view of him in his casket.

The demands of the next day's operation quickly removed that memory from my thoughts. Each day, in a war zone, demands full attention. But then there were other bodies to recover, living wounded to attend to and more war to experience. It has been said, "Nine tenths of war is waiting for the other tenth to happen," giving time for certain memories to return.

After nine months I contracted a terrible strain of malaria, removing over 40 pounds of my weight. I was left with an overall debilitating weakness. Back in my compound to recover, a strong force of communist troops attacked the next door army base, dictating we either fight or be removed from the area. Four of us were sent to a nearby air base for the duration of the battle, in which our side prevailed. In a few weeks I returned stateside, and then went home. My time in that war was over, but I did not return alone.

Within a few nights of peaceful sleep, I was awakened by the terrible memory of the body of the man on his way home the next day, and I was once again looking at his horrible head wound that had killed him. Only this time it morphed into the most horrible grotesque face I could imagine. I did not get back to sleep for quite a while. This became a too frequent event, not only disturbing that night's sleep, but often leaving me with a sluggish next day.

Coupled with this was my aversion to loud noises. No more enjoying the 4th of July, or hunting with my family. It was five years before I could finally shoot a gun. But the faces never stopped. Then a few years ago, I heard about the deliverance ministry and was immediately interested. I went thru it with Bob and Karen and was delivered from the memories and the faces! I thank my Lord Jesus I have not had a single night since deliverance where I was awakened by horrible memories of war or faces of the dead!

Deliverance is one of the most important and needed ministries our church offers and I implore all those with any demonic interference in their life to contact Bob or Karen, or a deliverance ministry near you for an opportunity to be set free!

#174...Fooling Herself

My name is Kelly.

I knew I needed to go through deliverance after my son and husband had gone through it. I saw something beautiful had happened in both of them. They both had a sense of peace that I had not seen in a long time and like a weight had been lifted off them, especially our son, like Scripture says, he was a new man; the old was gone. Really, both were like new men.

I had really never experienced what I thought as demonic activity in my life, nor devastating sin nor serious trauma, but I had my own designer baggage and it was filled with sinful behavior. A sin that comes to the front of my mind that I will share was that I would hold resentment against people. I would ruminate in my mind past hurts and I would create a new ending to what happened where I was esteemed and the bad people who hurt me were exposed for who they were and their lives would be miserable and mine great. Maybe to some people that behavior isn't anything to worry about, but think again, it is sin and a waste of time. It didn't add an ounce of anything positive to my life nor improve my life in any way. It was my secret sin and I hate to admit it, but I enjoyed doing it, especially when I would think about my husband's ex-wife.

But deliverance changed everything; it made me take a good thorough look at myself and it totally educated me on what God has to say about things we do and don't do. I would say to myself, "You have been a pretty good person, nothing too bad." Or, "My good totally outweighs the bad." I would excuse some of my sinful behavior as "Everyone does it." I excused little white lies to being OK. I thought if I never think about the sinful and hurtful things I have said and done, then all was OK.

All that changed through deliverance. It brought to my attention the need to confess ALL things that I had done in the past, even the things that I zipped tight in my personal baggage that I had never confessed before. I was with people who wanted only one thing for me and that was to be set free, to have that weight of past sins off of me. The Holy Spirit was working in me as my team went through each section of the deliverance folder. I could hear a voice saying, "You don't have to confess that." I could feel a knot in my throat like something caught in it that did not want to come out. I know that was a demon from the spiritual warfare that was being waged against me and for me. It wanted to stay in my life and torment me at its leisure, but it did not get its way! I felt demons leave me throughout my deliverance experience. I felt sin lifted off and away from me, just as it states in the book of Psalms 103:12, "…as far as east is from west so far does He remove our transgressions from us."

I know the enemy wants me to keep in the forefront of my mind all the things I have done wrong in my life; he wants to ruin my life and make me miserable and depressed. Demons' main goal is to kill and destroy us! I now have freedom that I believe happens only through deliverance and through this deliverance I have also learned how to stay free. I know that we aren't always fighting against flesh and blood and I now have the understanding and the power through the Holy Spirit to rebuke and cast away the thoughts that come to my mind, or behavior I don't want to be doing. I have the power to say, "Away from me in the name of JESUS." and it truly flees! I am free.

#175…Jester Spirit

One time we were doing deliverance on a young lady, and whenever we would try to call out a spirit which was tormenting her…A funny face would come on her (like a jester), laugh, and wag her finger toward us saying "Ha, ha, ha, you're not going to get me out." This went on for many sessions, and was so comical those of us ministering to her couldn't help but crack up. It was a definite distraction and actually hilarious!!! At times we laughed so hard we were crying…but we were not giving up.

Finally, God revealed to me that we needed to call the young lady back, and tell her what was going on and have her take authority over what we called 'jester spirit'… When she did that, the jester would shut up and the spirits of anger, rejection or whatever were able to be cast out. So for every session, we would have her address the 'jester spirit'…so she would say something like, "Jester spirit, in the name of Jesus, shut up and allow me to get these spirits out of me!" and the jester spirit shut up. We don't know for sure what that jester spirit was, but she got crazy deliverance, is witnessing to people, leading people to Jesus, has reconciled with family and is 'on fire' for Jesus now! Praise God from whom ALL blessings flow!!!

#176…Spoke In Tongues

My name is Alissa Cook.

I decided to go through deliverance after God led me to Bob & Karen's ministry. I actually had an encounter with a menacing demon that scared me, prompting me to seek help. When I explained my encounter to Karen, she informed me that she and her husband have a deliverance ministry & they invited me to Bible study.

I had already been praying & reading my Bible & became educated on what the Bible says about demons, so I decided to go through deliverance.

I had my suspicions on what demons I may have, but only one

manifested itself and it was the spirit of mockery. After it was cast out, I realized that I was afraid of being mocked for having faith in Jesus (Some of my family members - grandparents are very scientific.).

I witnessed a very dramatic deliverance in someone else over the course of the weekend [This is Bob...the incident she speaks of happened during one of the teachings when a demon manifested and then screamed out. It took about a minute or so to cast it out after the recipient had gone to the floor. See Luke 4:31-37. This can happen when the Word of God is taught with authority.].

Bob asked me if I wanted to speak in tongues by the power of the Holy Spirit. I said, "Yes," and I did it!

The Freedom Weekend was very impactful, and it was so awesome to see the authority of Jesus Christ displayed.

Thank you for your ever important prayers.

#177...Muslim No More

My name is Immanuel Matthew.

Early this year (February, 2016), I went to my hospital in Bangalore to care for a patient. I am a paid care-giver/attendant for patients. The patient's brother told me of a life-changing seminar of deliverance and inner-healing conducted by Pastor Larry. I was instantly interested and felt a deep desire to attend this seminar.

My patient's discharge from the hospital coincided with this seminar and we traveled to Hosur to attend this Deliverance and Inner Healing meeting.

The teaching classes were fabulous - a deep eye-opener for me. During the ministry deliverance sessions, I manifested demons. I was taken back and terrified. How could I, a devout Christian, have demons in me? But like other spiritual truths, this was open and real. Through careful and dedicated mentoring, I confessed my sins, forgave all those I needed to forgive, and those demons in me were cast out. I felt the presence of God and I felt connected. I took the water baptism and turned my back on my past faith and belief system, and I was christened as Immanuel Matthew.

I love my new being and my new name. This, in a nutshell, is my testimony. I feel a deep and burning passion to witness to my Muslim family and brethren. This is both challenging and maybe dangerous. But, it's got to be done! So please pray for me. Praise God! God is great!

#178…Couldn't Comprehend The Bible

We had a lady come to us who wasn't sure she had any spirits, however, she could not read the Bible or any Christian literature. She asked if that could be spirits. We never automatically assume it is demons but have the individual look at the situation from the lens of the Bible. We got further information from her, had her repent of some sin from her past, cut ungodly soul ties from the individuals who got her involved in the sins and forgive them, then we commanded any spirits associated with that sin to leave her in the name of Jesus. Her hands began shaking like crazy in a very animated manner, she cried and the spirits left. She commented she felt much lighter.

Later in the week, we got a text that she is now able to read and understand the Bible. Praise you Jesus!

#179…Two Hindus Converted

Brenda, a Hindu, came to the Transformation class because her sister, a Christian, had been to one previously and told her God could heal her of things. She was a corporate professional who had been "let go" from her high paying job recently and was full of bitterness and resentment.

Hephzibah, also a Hindu, was her 22 year old daughter who was in law school. She came because mom came. Both of them spoke English.

As was my mode of operation, as people were arriving the first day of the class, I asked the Lord who I should get to know. Then He pointed out Hephzibah to me. I looked at my wife and said, "See that young lady in the blue hoodie? We need to get to know her. She isn't a Christian."

I called our church back in the States and left a voice message for them to pray for "…a lady and her daughter in a blue hoodie. Something is going to happen."

On the first or second day, Hephzibah was standing by herself at lunch so we went over and introduced ourselves to her. We started learning about her and were glad to see she spoke English well. We also met Brenda soon thereafter and started building rapport with both of them.

Wednesday was the first group deliverance session. Just before it started, I felt two taps on my left shoulder. I looked and nobody was there...or anywhere close. I thought, "That must be an angel letting me know he's here." Later, this was confirmed to me. When deliverance started, I could see Hephzibah manifesting a spirit. I went over to her and spoke into her ear (It was loud in there!) and said, "Do you want me to cast it out in the name of Jesus?" She nodded in the affirmative. I said, "Jesus, show her that you are real. In the name of Jesus Christ, demon, come out!" She immediately coughed it out and a big smile of relief came over her face! I said, "It's gone!" and she nodded. Then I looked into her eyes and said, "Thank God you were delivered in the name of Jesus Christ."

Brenda, on the other hand, wanted nothing to do with this! She sat through each session with her arms folded and a scowl on her face! When screaming was going on, she would say, "They are hurting them!" Those around her would say, "No, those are demons screaming as they come out."

Every two days, I called the church back home and updated them with information like their names and that they were both Hindus.

The second week of the class, all the students are broken into small groups. To participate, one must be a Christian, so I said to Hephzibah, "You have been delivered of evil spirits by Jesus and you have seen many healed by Him. Are you ready to become a Christian?" Even though she had to deal with mom and her displeasure with it all, she said, "Yes!" So we prayed and she wholeheartedly confessed Jesus as Lord and believed God raised Him from the dead. She got saved!

Since Brenda wasn't a Christian, she couldn't participate in the group sessions, so I sent her to one of the rooms in the back with my wife and another American. My wife was not happy! She had to go back there with the "dragon lady," as she called her.

As soon as Hephzibah became a Christian, I went back to let the "dragon lady" know what had happened with her daughter. I said to her, "I want you to know that Hephzibah has just become a Christian." I braced for a furious response! "She did? Great!" Huh? What? I didn't expect that! Apparently, all the Word of God Brenda had heard had softened her heart and we hadn't noticed it.

I told Hephzibah about Brenda's response and she was delighted.

About ten minutes later, my wife came screaming into the room, "She just got saved!!" Yes, the dragon lady had gotten saved and the three of them stayed back there and Brenda also had many demons cast out of her by my wife and the other American! WOW!

As the class was ending, Hephzibah and Brenda, with big smiles on their faces, let me take a video of them and they thanked all the brothers and sisters and, especially, all the people back at our church for praying for them. God is good! Praise Him!

#180…Come Out Of Me!

A team of four of us ministered to Joy. Trent was on the team and he was her cousin. He took the lead since relatives have more authority than non-relatives.

As the weekend progressed, demons were coming out. In the final session, Joy's own determination and will came into play in a big way. The spirits that were left pushed her to the floor and she actually behaved like a giant lizard. We all were commanding the demons to come out in Jesus' name. Slowly, she began to speak to the spirits herself as we spoke less and less. She slowly moved from being flat on her face to up on her hands and knees, then one foot was on the floor, then two and her hands slowly went up into the air in triumph! In the end, she actually cast the final spirit out herself!

As she spoke more and more and we spoke less and less, this is how the words basically came out of her mouth, "You cannot stay here anymore! Jesus is my Lord and you are not welcome! You must go!" By this time we weren't saying anything, **"Come out of meeeeeee!!"** At this point, it left and she was free!

She is now a vital part of our deliverance teams and is giving those evil spirits a lot of, shall we say, payback! Praise the Lord!

#181…Up The Fireplace

Bobby was a big dude and came from Alabama for deliverance. Once upon a time he had played college football under Alabama's Coach Bear Bryant. Geoff and I were about to coach him a different way!

As we progressed through deliverance, the Lord showed us, bit by bit, what we needed to know. During one of the sessions, I "saw" in the spirit, a black blob in his lungs. I asked Bobby about this and he didn't know what it was. As we continued, we commanded the "black blob" to come out. In a later session, Bobby said he could see what looked like an octopus in his own lungs. So, we changed from casting out the black blob to the "octopus." Still later, while we were commanding spirits out that were coughing energetically as they came out, Geoff asked,

"WOW! Did you see that?" "No," I said, to which Geoff responded, "I just saw a small black thing, about the size of a quarter with a tail about six inches long, come out of his mouth, go to the chimney and up it!" We determined that the black blob octopus was really a bunch of little spirits intertwined that were coming out one at a time.

Was it cancer? We don't know. We did know that he had been a smoker years earlier. We also knew that it all came out. Praise the Lord!

By the way, Bobby told us that Coach Bear Bryant used to stand in a tower and watch while the assistant coaches conducted practices at Alabama. One day, a player was defiantly mouthing off to one of the coaches. Coach Bryant yelled down, "Get off my practice field and don't ever come back!" Bobby never saw him again!

#182…Murder Trauma

We did deliverance on a very sweet young lady in her 20's. She had served God since she was 7 and had lived a very godly life. So we were surprised when we casually mentioned the spirit of murder and she went flying backward and froze like the crime scene outline of where a person has been murdered… she didn't move for what seemed like an eternity! (I remember turning to Bob and saying, "Did we kill her?").

We were finally able to call her (the young lady) back to consciousness and asked her about it. We learned she had previously worked in a police crime lab documenting murders (she could tell you where different body parts had been found all over the county where she worked). Through the trauma from working those crime scenes, the murder spirit had gotten into her! Trauma can bring spirits into a person! We there were able to break soul ties and cast that spirit out of her.

#183…He That Is In You Is Greater

When I am asked to preside over a funeral and/or memorial service, I accept, as I will take every opportunity to proclaim the name of Jesus. This particular service was no exception to that rule. From the moment I stepped into the pulpit, my heart became heavy for several in attendance. I saw hollow eyes and blank stares during this service, instead of life-giving eyes.

As I began to share the Gospel with those present, a man stood up in the back right corner and yelled, "No!" Without hesitation, I continued to share the life-changing message of Jesus, focusing on

His teachings, crucifixion, and resurrection. As the Holy Spirit began to move, silence swept the chapel, and the man who had spoken out sat down and remained silent. The eyes that had been cast down were suddenly looking up and toward me.

Following the service, the same gentleman asked if he could speak with me in private. I responded, "Sure." As we made our way to the side porch of the chapel, he reached in his pocket, pulled out a switchblade knife, held it to my throat, and said, "I am going to cut you." Without a blink of an eye or a tremor in my voice, I responded, "In the name of Jesus, what is inside of me is stronger than what has a hold of you." He dropped the knife as though it was hot and he could no longer grasp it. As I reached down to pick it up, he said, "Don't touch it; there are demons all over it." He then began to cry and asked why I was compassionate to him.

We must never underestimate the power that the name of Jesus holds. For this, I am thankful.

#184…Schizophrenia?

We had a mental health professional where we live contact us about a client. The therapist felt that although the client, in her 30's, had been diagnosed with schizophrenia with hallucinations, there seemed to be something else going on. The client was a Christian and thought so also. We agreed to meet with the client and see if we could be of help.

Upon getting together, we realized there were many things going on in her and her family's lives. After learning their stories, having them repent, break ungodly soul ties and forgive others, we commanded any spirits in her to go away and never return. After a short time, we heard back from the lady that all of the issues were gone, and then we lost contact with her.

We saw the therapist probably one year later, who told us that the woman was totally healed; she is off of her schizophrenia medication, and no longer needing therapy. About 5 years later the lady sent us an e-mail, thanking us and telling us how awesome her life was and how victorious she is still living, newly married and having a full and stable life. Praise Jesus!

#185…Snidely Whiplash

A fellow minister and I were praying for Billy and I "saw" in the Spirit a short man with a big hat and curly mustache. It wasn't a clear picture, but it was just "there." Now, in the past, I would have ignored this, thinking that something was in my Diet Coke earlier! But I've learned to go with whatever I see and more times than not, it will be from the Lord. The picture reminded me of the Disney character, Yosemite Sam, only the mustache was more like Snidely Whiplash.

I said, "I see a small man with a big hat and mustache." I couldn't quite put what I was thinking into words and then my partner, speaking by the Spirit of God, said, "Have you been mischievous in the past?" I said, "That's it!" Billy affirmed that he had been very much that way as a kid and would get in trouble in school because of it. This carried over into his adult life as well. So, he confessed his sin and cut any ungodly soul ties with the people he was mischievous with (that he could remember) and then we cast the mischievous spirit out of him through coughing.

#186…Shaken Inside

My name is Jebasing Paulraj.
When I came to this meeting, I came with the mind that hereafter there won't be any progress at all in my life. I had gone to many spiritual meetings, and I was not able to see change in my life. So to this meeting also I came, with the plan of being there 10 days to eat and sleep well. I was making 0% progress in my spiritual life when I came here.

I was carrying a lot of depression both spiritually and physically. But on the first day, when Daddy prayed the closing prayer, I could see a black thing leaving me. From the second day onwards, I could see a desire for God's Word and began to receive it.

In other meetings, I used to watch demons leaving from other people. But here, I myself began to receive deliverance from many foul demons. After each deliverance, I received freshness and could feel joy increasing in me.

This camp really shook my life. I received light into my heart. During the Holy Spirit ministry, I received a great healing into my unconscious realm. I was delivered inside me greatly. All glory to God.

#187…Hibernating Spirit

My name is Joel Lawson.
I Just wanted to say "Thank you" to you and the team for this

weekend's deliverance.

I came in with an open mind knowing that I may have something hiding within. I feel I have received relief from the sorrow I still felt from my brother's death back in 1989. As I suspected, I did in fact have a hibernating/hidden spirit. The team members picked up on it on day 2. With some research we were able to figure it out and cast it out on day 3. I feel good about the whole experience and look forward to moving on from all my past.

#188...No More Faking It

My name is Lyman Shawn Bowling.

I was 13 years old when I asked Jesus into my heart. At 16, I put God on a shelf for when I needed him.

I met my wife when I was around 19 years old and we were married within 6 months. I was living for myself and did all that made me feel happy. I was always trying to make my wife feel happy, but really not caring about her happiness over mine. We had 6 children within 8 years.

Years later, we had heard about deliverance through our daughter's in-laws. They had gone on a mission trip and were completely changed when they got back. So, my wife said she wanted to start going to the same Bible study they were going to. So, to make her HAPPY, I agreed. In February, 2018, they had a group deliverance weekend. I went to make her happy. I did not believe in it, nor did I really participate in this weird religious stuff.

About half way through Saturday afternoon, there were LOUD NOISES AND SCREAMING coming from the room that the women were in. Bob said to me, "Shawn, your wife needs you!!!" I responded, NO SHE DOESN'T!!! I'M GOOD RIGHT HERE... There was no way I was going into that room.

I kept on living my life the way I had been: going to church, checking all the boxes on Sunday morning and so on. So, about 3 years after that weekend, I finally wanted to get right with God. I wanted to let go of the way I was living my life and let God be in control. I asked Bob if I could go through the next deliverance weekend and he said "Yes." So, I went to it.

This time I was willing to let go and be freed from my past experiences that I was dragging and holding on to. I was set free. Now God is using me to help others to be able to let go of their past baggage and be set free as well. To watch someone let go and forgive in order to release the things that has kept them separated from our Father's love, and to see them be able to get to a point that they are able to crawl into The FATHER'S LAP AND BE HELD is AWESOME.

This is why I am telling my story: to share my heart's desire to see others be set free. To God be the Glory.

#189...Repent For Freedom

I had many dealings with demons from the outside, in dreams, and in several houses over the past 37 years. However, it wasn't until fall 2021 that I ever considered it was possible to have demons inside me.

Truthfully, I went through deliverance so I could be a part of the ministry. I was very surprised the first time one rose up inside me. It was during the teaching session on forgiveness. I had to go to the restroom quickly and spit it out. That was such a relief. After that I was determined to look under every rock, so to speak, in order to get fully clean. The final morning at home I prayed. I declared out loud that I belonged to King Jesus!

I had repented for the past two days and reaffirmed that. I rushed to get into my car for the 45 minute drive to the church. Suddenly it dawned on me, "I can get that sucker out." You see, I felt something else was hiding...it was like a blockage. I yelled at the top of my voice for it to come out. Then it started coming....where to spit? Where to spit? I turned my head to the left and out it came on the window. I pulled over and cleaned up the car window and what got on me. I was going to be late now. But I WAS FREE! I understood at that moment what it meant that Jesus came to set the captives free.

I am keeping myself free day by day. I'm learning to be obedient to God, believing in the Bible as 100% reliable. Truth and righteousness are the keys to being free. They are the keys to spiritual warfare too. "The weapons of our warfare are not carnal...." Until I put to use my faith and understood how practical and useful it is, I was hampered.

You have to believe although you do not see! (Hebrews 11:1)
You know! Use the weapons and believe!

#190...One Is Greater Than Many

I have been in the deliverance ministry actively for about 20 years. One of the most amazing sessions I have ever been a part of was the first "mass" deliverance I ever conducted in Winchester, VA. I had just heard Derek Prince teach on this and heard him do a session where everyone expels demons simultaneously after they have repented, closed all doors and then they throw them out. As soon as I heard Derek Prince do one, I knew that I was next.

It was during a session of a class that I teach called *Exercising Spiritual Authority* and no one, including myself, knew what to expect when, after teaching, I finally gave the word and demanded that all the demons leave the people. Not only was it mass deliverance, it was mass pandemonium (which means "all demons."). People started heaving and throwing up; some were tossed all about the room, and one guy began rolling around on the floor knocking people down and creating all sorts of commotion when he was banging into chairs and tables. There I stood in front of the people, with my mouth gaping wide open, not knowing what to do next.

I had the presence of mind to take control of the situation and began working with each person that was manifesting. The Holy Spirit showed me that the people who were manifesting the expulsion of these demons still had places of authority that needed repentance. Slowly, one by one, I cast out each demon that was still hanging on. I had never seen such things before. We had healings and deliverances and testimonies for quite a while.

I walked away from that experience knowing emphatically that the name of Jesus Christ frightens demons and that I really had been given authority over demons as the Bible says. Since then I have conducted hundreds of mass deliverances around the world and am still amazed at the power and authority given to man through the Holy Spirit.

#191…Crawling Gunslinger

It was the first group deliverance session in the Transformation class and a man was sitting next to the isle. As the leader commanded spirits out, I commanded them out in this man. The demon didn't like it and tried to get away. It made the man to walk on all fours down the aisle ever so slowly. As this happened, I stayed with him and continued to command the demon out. After about 15 feet of progress, the spirit finally left and the man fell into a heap on the floor. Moments later, he got up and by his expressions I could tell he hoped no one had seen him. Then he went back to his seat and quietly sat down.

The scene reminded me of a wild west movie where the two gunslingers fire at each other. One is wounded and tries desperately to crawl away while the other one stands over him, waiting for the right moment to finish him off! When it comes, he pulls the trigger and puts him out of his misery!

It must be awful to be a demon, knowing you are an eternal loser!

Chapter 15
Minimal Results

Can we be honest? Can we tell stories that didn't end like we would have liked? When things don't go the way we would like, we learn for the next time. We don't wallow in self-condemnation, but get up and keep going. That's what Peter did and he is the poster child for mistakes made in the Bible.

On the other hand, less than the best results don't necessarily mean we did anything wrong.

We don't know for sure how much good we do at times. Perhaps we plant seeds of success in some of them and God will bring fruit later.

Live and learn.

#192...Epilepsy Spirit

I was ministering in Ecuador when a thirteen year old girl was brought to me. She had epilepsy. The ministry time we had was very short, like maybe 10 minutes, so I had to hurry. I began to command the spirit out and quickly it started to manifest. This hadn't happened to her before and it scared her. I tried to put her at ease, but she sort of shut down and wanted to discontinue and since her mom felt the same, we stopped.

Would I have done anything differently if I could turn back the clock? I don't know what it would be. Perhaps, since her mom now knew that the issue is a demon, she got deliverance later. I don't know, but I did the best I could in the moment and love never fails.

#193...He Speaks English?

I was translating for a youth group mission team in a park in Nuevo Laredo Mexico, just across the border from Laredo Texas. We had just performed a set of dramas sharing the Gospel of Jesus with those that had gathered to watch. During the presentation, I noticed a man among a crowd. I knew instantly that he was demon possessed and I did not want to go over and talk to him. We found out later that his name was Victor.

I was translating for a high school team and one of them asked me to come translate for him. He headed in the opposite direction than where Victor was so I was glad that we weren't going toward him. As soon as I agreed to go with him, he turned on his heels and went straight for Victor who was a homeless man. He was sitting on the ground calmly but looked out of his mind.

When we got over there, we were trying to communicate with him and the young teenager didn't have a clue that he was demon possessed. He looked very worn and was in his mid-thirties to forty.

The teen knew Victor needed a touch from God and was reiterating what we had shared in the dramas about Christ and they exchanged names. We spoke with him for a few minutes, but when we asked him if he wanted to receive Jesus, something changed in Victor, including his voice, and the teenager fell back on his heels, looked at me and asked, "What did he say?" Because he didn't sound like the guy we had just been talking to. I said, "OK, just pray in tongues." To which he replied, "I don't know how to pray in tongues." So I told him to just pray.

I took over the conversation at that point and spoke in Spanish and told the demon that I wanted to talk to Victor now, right now, and commanded the demon, in Jesus' name, to let me talk to Victor. Victor then came back to the forefront. He knew something had happened, but he didn't know what. It was like he was asleep and then he would kind of wake up and then it would be him again. This happened several times. Any time we would get really direct about making a decision to pray with us, the demon would come back and take over the moment and refuse any compliance. I told Victor, when he was back, that this was his choice.

At one point the demon started talking to us in English. The teenager freaked out and said, "He [Victor] speaks English?" I told him that it wasn't Victor. I knew that talking to the demon was not at all what I wanted to do except for commanding him to let Victor make a decision for himself.

Ultimately, he made the decision that he didn't want to accept Jesus at that time so he didn't get delivered. He didn't want to really entertain what we had taught about freedom in Christ or liberty in

Jesus. He didn't want any of that, so we had to walk away.

We talked with him for at least 20 minutes. We felt somewhat defeated, but at the same time we knew we had done what we needed to do in the moment we had for Victor to hear and have the opportunity. It was his choice.

#194...Hit Man

Bruce was supposed to arrive from out-of-state at 9:00 AM. At exactly 8:00 the power went out in our home for maybe five seconds. Then the phone rang, "I'm here and I'm in the driveway." We thought, "The show is about to start!"

This deliverance was unlike any we had taken part in. Bruce was jumpy, scary (my wife hid the knives), was wanting to be on his phone constantly, was bitter from his divorce and he told us he tried to hire a hit man to kill his wife, "Hit men aren't as expensive as you might think," he said.

At one point I told him, "Make up your mind. You are either here for deliverance or you need to leave. That means I don't want to see your phone again." He stayed.

I remember he got great freedom during the rejection session. He cried a lot so we knew that spirits were leaving through his tears.

Later, we heard from the man who referred him to us and he told us that he was like a new person! He got very involved in church, was friendly, had lost his hatred toward his ex-wife, and his relationships with others became so positive. He was totally different.

Eventually, he didn't return our emails and we lost contact with him. We did hear from our contact person, several years later, who told us what happened. Bruce had gone back to his old ways and was arrested when he tried to hire a hit man who was an informant. While awaiting trial, he went to the home of his ex-wife and started shooting a gun at it. Her new husband, aware of the threats, had a gun for protection and shot and killed Bruce.

We are not transformed by having demons cast out of us. We are transformed by abiding in His Word and then God transforms us from the inside. Bruce didn't let this happen.

#195...Black Spiders

Sunan was a Christian who had cancer. She said to me one day,

"I know what is in me is evil; will you cast it out?" "Of course!" As we ministered to her, I knew there were people she needed to forgive, and she did. As we commanded spirits out, she coughed them out, but strained to get others out. They were there, and she could tell they were there, but they did not come out.

At this time, I had a vision of black spiders on a spider web that was made of steel. It was like a screen door or window. The spiders represented demons. Some of them were on the outside and left when commanded to do so. But, most of them were on the inside and could not get out because the steel web was holding them in. I told her what I was seeing and explained it to her. Then I said, "Something is holding these demons in. Is there anything you're not telling us?" She said, "No."

A few months later, Sunan died. Just before she passed away, she revealed to family members that a mutual acquaintance had raped her and this was verified. I found out about it some time later. She had her golden opportunity to tell us about the rape when the Lord gave me the vision, but she didn't. Would she have been healed of cancer? I can't honestly say although I think so.

Why did she hide the rape? Sunan immigrated to the USA from Iraq along with many family members. In Iraq, if you rape a loved one, you had better be a fast runner and good hider, because they will be coming for you and after they find you, the police will look the other way when you exact revenge. She was afraid of what they would do if she told the truth. In addition, the raper threatened her if she told anybody. Her fears were well founded because they, shall we say, ultimately made him very "uncomfortable."

Sunan did not want to tell us the truth and God did not override her will. To receive deliverance, one must be totally honest to receive God's best.

#196…Waste Of Time?

Bubba came for deliverance, or so we thought. He really came to satisfy his wife who wanted him to come. He went through the motions and did what we said, but we could tell he was just playing the game. Near the end I said, "I'm worried about your salvation because you don't seem to care about how you have hurt your wife! I don't see any remorse or real desire to change!" His response was that he did care blah blah blah blah. If you do deliverance long enough, you can tell when someone really wants it and is sincere and when it just isn't there.

It wasn't there.

Yes, demons came out of him through coughing, but only superficial ones. The real biggies were safe and sound on the inside hiding behind his facade of wanting it. I felt like it was a waste of time, but, I hope I'm wrong.

#197…Sad Ending

Joe was brought to us by a friend from another city about 75 miles away for deliverance. Phil, my wife and I ministered to him. We spent a few hours with him and got some demons out, but we all felt that something was missing. We weren't sure what, but we knew we should have had better results.

That night the three of us had weird dreams. I dreamt I was married to a man and I was running around trying to figure out how to get a divorce. Phil called me the next day and said he had a dream that he was having sex with a man. My wife had a similar, homosexual dream. I called my friend and told him that if Joe wants to come back for more deliverance, he needs to confess and repent of his homosexual activity. We never heard back from Joe, although my friend did tell us that same sex relationships were an issue for him.

About a year later I found out that Joe had committed suicide. As it turns out, a suicidal tendency was another secret Joe didn't reveal to us.

#198…Take Me Home

Dorothy was excited to be receiving deliverance. She just knew it was going to be great. She even said that she hoped to be doing deliverance herself soon. She really needed it since she had many torments.

At the end of the first session, we were doing the prayers and had her repeating them after us. It was supposed to be something like this, "Heavenly Father, I forgive all those who have hurt me. I forgive…" and she was to name people she was to forgive. Instead, she said, "Jesus, help me forgive…" She was putting the duty to forgive on Jesus, when the Word of God says to just do it. Moments earlier, we had taught on this very thing from the Bible. We gently corrected her by saying that it was up to her and she just needed to forgive, but she refused to do it. As we pondered what to do next, she said, "Take me home." Again, we didn't just want to give up, but hesitated and tried to hear the Lord's voice as to what we should do. Then she said, "Do I need to call the police?"

One of our team members took her home and we never heard from her or saw her again.

#199...Sexting

Several of us were ministering to Tanner. Small demons were coming out, but we could tell that Tanner wasn't being completely honest with us. The results were limited.

One of the issues was that one of his friends had a former girlfriend who, while she was his girlfriend, texted naked photos of herself to him. He showed them to Tanner and another guy after they had broken up. They told her they would spread the photos all over the college campus if she didn't have sex with each one of them (small campus where everybody knew each other).

He wouldn't say any more about it. We knew he had extorted sex from her, but he wouldn't admit it, or anything else that needed to be admitted.

The girl ended up leaving the school.

The last thing I said to him was that unless he would repent of what he had done, there was nothing more we could do for him. He didn't.

#200...Suicide Torments

We were ministering in a remote village in Mexico. After preaching Christ, and seeing many saved, we offered healing in Jesus' name. I saw a woman and sensed that suicide was an issue for her. I approached her gently and asked, "Quieres que te ministremos?" (Do you want us to minister to you?) She nodded in the affirmative. I said, "Tienes malos pensamientos?" (Do you have bad thoughts?) She again nodded. "Piensas en el suicidio?" (Do you think of suicide?) Then she began to weep uncontrollably while nodding in the affirmative.

Another believer joined me as we ministered to her. We found out when it started and what she needed to confess and who she needed to forgive. As we prayed and commanded the suicide spirits out, she had some relief, but we could tell there was more work to be done. Our time was short and we were not going to return and as people began to crowd around, including her relatives, she shut down. She was more concerned with what people, especially relatives, would think if they knew she was suicidal than getting set free. Our efforts quickly ceased after this.

We never saw her again.

Conclusion
Now What?

Some of you may be thinking, this is crazy, I'm not sure about this, I've never been taught this, and my denomination doesn't support this, etcetera.

To be totally transparent...I (Karen) was among the chief of skeptics of transformation/deliverance. I am a mental health provider and I use evidence based methods to try to help individuals in their goal to improve their mental health, relationships, and so on. I told Bob, "you can do deliverance and I will counsel them afterwards." Yes, I was a skeptic...but as I began to minister with Bob, I saw miracles before my eyes of transformed lives...I would have never believed it if I hadn't seen it...demons speaking in my language to me (when the person knew no English), people's bodies manifesting in the ways that are described in the Bible and in this book. I've seen it and I've seen Christians who were previously in bondage to sins they couldn't seem to break, such as sex addictions, anger, extreme anxiety, and more, totally delivered and freed. Much to my excitement, yet contrary to my professional counseling experiences, I saw many individuals who had previously been under treatment with mental health professionals, no longer need mental health care. They are free from bondage! They now are on fire for God and sharing the gospel...I've seen it and know the Bible of 'yesterday' is totally applicable today. (Once again, we never tell people to stop mental health care, or discontinue their psychotropic medications!)

I'm reminded of the woman with the issue of blood...she defied religious tradition, and training, and cultural norms to touch Jesus, and be healed (Mark 5:24-34, Luke 8:42-28). This is my challenge to you: pray about getting out of your fears, religion, denominational boundaries and preconceived notions, and start being Jesus to those who are hurting. If you are not knowledgeable or comfortable offering freedom and deliverance to those who are hurting in your sphere of influence, find someone who can and will cast out the darkness in their lives through the power and authority in Jesus name!

I am so burdened that we have people, in our churches, medical practices, businesses, spheres of influence in general, who are: self-harming, suicidal and depressed…who need help! These individuals are tormented, and many of them have been in and out of mental hospitals, psychiatrist offices and therapy offices, they are medicated with anti-psychotics, antidepressants and other mind-altering medications to help them survive. Many are using marijuana and alcohol just to cope with life. Many families have come to us…frustrated because the church's answer was to pray, and go to their doctor or a counselor, which have not provided the help they needed. God's word addresses self harm and suicide as being from the enemy (Ephesians 5:29). And the demoniac, who lived among the tombs, is the first example in the Bible of someone who was a 'cutter' (Matthew 8:28-34, Mark 5:1-20, Luke 8:26-39).

Families with discord in their homes are also a place for deliverance. The enemy comes to steal, kill and destroy, and he loves to destroy our homes through unforgiveness, bitterness, and abuse. We have found that when couples go through a Freedom Weekend, their home lives improve! Their homes become a place of increased forgiveness and unity, becoming a more accurate reflection of Jesus and His love!

All of these individuals are living out Ephesians 6:12: "For we wrestle not against flesh and blood, but against principalities, against powers, against the rulers of the darkness of this world, against spiritual wickedness in high places" (KJV).

Jesus is the answer…He gave us the power and authority to trample over demons, to heal those who are oppressed of the devil: "And these signs will accompany those who believe: In my name they will drive out devils…" (Mark 16:17 NKJV)

God calls us to do this: "…God anointed Jesus of Nazareth with the Holy Ghost and with power: who went about doing good, and healing all that were oppressed of the devil; for God was with him…"(Acts 10:38 NKJV).

And God's Word affirms we can do this as followers of Jesus! "Most assuredly, I say to you, he who believes in Me, the works that I do he will do also; and greater works than these he will do, because I go to My Father" (John 14:12 NKJV).

We look back at all of the transformed lives and are moved to tears. We have been so incredibly blessed to see numerous people set free through God's working through the freedom ministry we have been blessed to oversee.

How Can We Be Sure It Works?

First, God's Word proclaims it.

Second, throughout this book you have true examples of how people's lives have been dramatically changed by being freed of evil spirits. These are people who had accepted Jesus as their Lord and Savior, yet were in bondage to their past and unable to move forward in the things of God. These individuals now live the full and abundant life God promises, and they are also leading others to Jesus through their transformed lives of power in Christ.

I am terribly burdened that the church as a whole is missing out on helping these hurting individuals. Please pray and seek God and be open to providing, and or recommending, deliverance though Jesus to the hurting individuals in your life and church. I know this is "out of the box" for many of you…it was totally out of the box for this 'mainstream church girl,' but I thank God for revealing His truth to me so I have been to help so many individuals, and see God do "..exceedingly abundantly more than I could ever hope or think, according to the power that works in us…" (Ephesians 3:20-21 NKJV).

Yes, people need to "…be not conformed to this world but be transformed by the renewing of your mind, that you may prove what is that good and acceptable and perfect will of God" (Romans 12:2 KJV). Understand though, that often trauma, abuse, and sin have allowed the enemy to attack these individuals in such a way that they cannot "prove what is that good and acceptable and perfect will of God" until these evil spirits are cast out of or away from them.

So I'm encouraging you to recognize the solution is in transformation and deliverance and please be willing to tell those you love, your church family, your clients and your patients about this healing from Jesus! Be willing to find someone who will walk this journey with them…we can't try to placate these families with religiosity, they need the healing from Jesus…it's through the transforming power of God's Word. I'm not saying there is not a place for medical interventions, therapy, etcetera. However, God is the true healer and producer of transformed lives!

I'M SICK OF THE ENEMY STEALING THE JOY AND PEACE AND FREEDOM GOD INTENDED US TO HAVE! I'm sick of seeing Christians cycling in and out of emergency rooms, crisis centers and mental hospitals due to mental illness…I see them. I hate Satan stealing the freedom that believers should be able to live!!!!

ABOUT THE AUTHORS

Robert (Bob) has a B.A. in History from Michigan State University, a M.S. in Bible Theology and Christian Ministries from Great Lake Christian College, and a Master of Arts in Religion: Biblical Studies from Liberty Theological Seminary and Graduate School.

In his 45 years of Christian service, Bob has pastored churches and has preached, ministered deliverance, and taught classes in spiritual authority in the United States, Asia, Mexico, Central America and South America. Bob previously authored *Ekballo: What the Bible Teaches About Every Christian's Authority Over the Evil Spirit Realm.*

Karen has a B.A. of Sociology from Mid-America Nazarene University, M.A. in Corporate Communication from Western Kentucky University, and a M.A. in Professional Counseling from Liberty University. She has served as a Bible study teacher and in leadership with Christian organizations. She is a Licensed Professional Clinical Counselor when not traveling and ministering with Bob. She has also ministered in the United States, Asia, Mexico, Central America and South America.

Bob and Karen are not "denominational loyalists" but have been members of/or attended Presbyterian, United Methodist, In-Home, Congregational, Church of Christ, Assembly of God, Baptist, Southern Baptist, Church of God, Nazarene and Independent Churches. Both Bob and Karen are ordained ministers.

If you are interested in having a weekend conference in your city, or wish to discuss personal ministry needs. You can contact Bob and Karen through Shattered Shackles.com or shatteredshacklesministry@gmail.com.

Bibliography

Capps, Charles, 1976. *The Tongue, A Creative Source*, 14th printing. Harrison House.

Hammond, Frank & Hammond, Ida Mae, 2010. *Pigs In the Parlor: The Practical Guide to Deliverance,* Impact Christian Books.

Hammond, Robert J., 2011. *Ekballo: What the Bible Teaches About Every Christian's Authority Over the Evil Spirit Realm*, 3rd Edition, This Moment Publishers.

Holy Bible: The King James Version, 1989. Tyndale House Publishers, Inc.

Holy Bible: The New King James Version, 1993. Thomas Nelson Publishers.

McIlhaney, Joe S., Jr. & McKissick Bush, Freda. 2008. *Hooked: New Science on How Casual Sex is Affecting our Children,* Northfield Publishing

Sides, Dale M., 2002. *Mending Cracks in the Soul: The Role of the Holy Spirit in Healing Wounds of the Past,* Liberating Publications, Inc.